Arguments for Welfare

Rowman & Littlefield International— Policy Impacts

The Rowman & Littlefield International—Policy Impacts series aims to bridge the gap between the academic community and policymakers: providing academics with a format and channel for policy-relevant research and ensuring that policymakers are informed about the best research available to them. Rowman & Littlefield International—Policy Impacts provides a forum for knowledge exchange, a bank of information and a toolkit for implementation.

Titles in the Series:

Arguments for Welfare

The Welfare State and Social Policy

Paul Spicker

ROWMAN &
LITTLEFIELD
————INTERNATIONAL

London • New York

Published by Rowman & Littlefield International Ltd
Unit A, Whitacre Mews, 26-34 Stannary Street, London SE11 4AB
www.rowmaninternational.com

Rowman & Littlefield International Ltd. is an affiliate of Rowman & Littlefield
4501 Forbes Boulevard, Suite 200, Lanham, Maryland 20706, USA
With additional offices in Boulder, New York, Toronto (Canada), and Plymouth (UK)
www.rowman.com

British Library Cataloguing in Publication Data
A catalogue record for this book is available from the British Library

ISBN: HB 978-1-78660-301-2
         PB 978-1-78660-302-9

Library of Congress Cataloging-in-Publication Data
ISBN 978-1-78660-301-2 (cloth: alk. paper)
ISBN 978-1-78660-302-9 (pbk: alk. paper)
ISBN 978-1-78660-303-6 (electronic)

♾™ The paper used in this publication meets the minimum requirements of American
National Standard for Information Sciences—Permanence of Paper for Printed Library
Materials, ANSI/NISO Z39.48-1992.

Printed in the United States of America

Contents

Chapter One

Understanding the Welfare State

Some arguments are so obvious that no-one makes them. There is not much discussion about whether people should live in families, whether children should be educated, whether people should be able to buy food or whether there should be laws. There may be those who take a different view, but they are on the fringes. Their positions will be reviewed in passing, discussed in academic circles and occasionally someone experiments with alternatives, but the alternatives are not taken very seriously. The world we live in is taken for granted.

The provision of social welfare is different. On one hand, nearly every developed society is engaged to some degree with the issues of social protection. There are commonly occurring patterns of social need, and there is a constellation of benefits and services, typically covering old age, ill health and the interruption of earnings. Many independent groups and organisations have made arrangements for the provision of welfare, and in general there are complex, overlapping networks through which services are delivered. Beyond that, in every democratic society, government has also come to play a role in provision, sometimes providing services directly, but almost invariably recognising that it has some responsibility for the direction of welfare policy.

On the other hand, and despite the very generality of these arrangements, there is a chorus of dissent. The main focus of criticism has been about the idea that government should be involved at all. Many of the basic precepts of economic theory seem to argue against collective provision and distribution of goods. Arguments made against state welfare for hundreds of years – that people who receive welfare are a burden on others, that welfare encourages idleness, that it is wasteful – are frequently repeated, usually with the claim that even if welfare worked in the past, this time it's different. Often welfare

1

systems are deeply resented. If we need to be reminded why we ought to have welfare, it is because so many people have come to think that we should not.

THE WELFARE STATE

There are some widespread misconceptions about welfare, but it will be difficult even to discuss the issue without at least a shared vocabulary. The first problem lies with the term 'welfare' itself. Economists use the term to refer generally to people's well-being, but that is not the main subject here. Part of the general argument for a welfare state is an argument for making things better. However, lots of things make people's lives better – music, comedy, open countryside, books, gardening, shopping, dancing or messing around in boats – and welfare states do not have much to do with any of them. There are publicly funded activities in many countries which help people do some of these things – public broadcasters, parks, sports grounds, libraries and community theatres – and they are almost certainly better places to live because of it, because then people have choices for a good life that they would not otherwise have. This is not, however, the stuff that welfare states are made of. The main use of the word 'welfare' refers instead to the provision of a conventional range of services – systems that have been developed to safeguard vulnerable people in a range of contingencies. The activities of welfare states are typically concerned with health, social security, housing, education, employment support and social care. The people who are being supported, typically pensioners, children, people with disabilities and those who are unemployed, are people who have been identified as having needs that ought to be met through collective social arrangements.

Even within that discourse, people understand the terms differently. The dominant use of the term 'welfare' in the United States is focused on a relatively narrow group of services, mainly concerned with people of working age on very low incomes. That sense was hardly used in Europe fifteen or twenty years ago, but it has become more and more prevalent, especially in Britain. The most obvious difference in definitions is that the broader sense of the term includes provision for medical care, pensions, education, housing support and social care. It is not difficult to defend welfare in the narrow sense as well as in a broader sense, but quite apart from the arbitrariness of the definition, the restriction of the argument has had some pernicious effects. One is the deliberate separation of arguments for welfare where the legitimacy of public provision is generally accepted from others where it is not: publicly funded schooling is usually approved of, support for low-income families with children often is not. A second example is the distinction drawn between arguments for pensions and arguments for support for younger people who are unable to work, often presented as a difference between the 'deserving' and 'undeserving'. There are few arguments for offering people a pension at sixty-five that cannot be made for supporting unemployed people aged fifty-eight. These distinctions create problems for practice too. Services which are confined to residual, stigmatised groups tend equally to be stigmatised, complex and expensive, and treated as a 'public burden', and arguments against 'welfare' in these terms tend to be self-fulfilling.

The idea of the 'welfare state' is no clearer. Titmuss complained that it was an "indefinable abstraction".[1] At times, the idea seems to be used to describe any arrangements that happen to be made. If all modern states are welfare states, Veit-Wilson complains, the word 'welfare' is not saying anything – "the term 'welfare' becomes redundant and mystifying noise."[2]

The idea of the welfare state originated in Bismarck's Germany. The German system after Bismarck was a scheme of insurance for people who worked, and it hardly concerned itself with the poorest at all. The Beveridge report in the United Kingdom,[3] although it was mainly concerned with the development of a national insurance scheme, was taken to represent an ideal system of government[4] where people were provided for as a right of citizenship[5] and covered 'from the cradle to the grave'. The French system, sometimes thought of as a fusion of principles from Bismarck and Beveridge,[6] actually did something quite different: aiming to include as many people as possible in solidaristic and mutualist schemes, but tending to leave out those at the bottom, the 'excluded', until the system was reformed in the 1980s. The Swedish system, which for many has become paradigmatic of what a welfare state could achieve, used mutualist and occupational structures to pursue objectives of solidarity and social equality.

The academic literature on welfare states often describes them in terms of normative models. The best-known example, though there are lots of others, is the work of Gøsta Esping-Andersen. Esping-Andersen classifies three main types of 'welfare régime'. The 'liberal' regimes, including the United States and the United Kingdom, are market-oriented and offer welfare on a residual basis, as a safety net, in the assumption that most people will deal with issues through their own resources. The corporatist regimes, such as Germany

---

1. R. Titmuss, 1968, Commitment to welfare, London: Allen and Unwin, p. 124.
2. J. Veit-Wilson, 2000, States of welfare, Social Policy and Administration 34(1), 1–25, p. 3.
3. Cmd 6404, 1942, Social insurance and allied services, London: HMSO.
4. A. Briggs, 1961, The welfare state in historical perspective, European Journal of Sociology 2, 221–58.
5. T. H. Marshall, 1982, The right to welfare, London: Heinemann.
6. For example, B. Palier and G. Bonoli, 1995, Entre Bismarck et Beveridge, Revue Française de Science Politique 45(4), 668–99.

and France, have pressed welfare into the service of the economy, organising its delivery through integrating it with representations of employers, trades unions and other key agencies. The social democratic regimes, exemplified by the Scandinavian countries, have 'decommodified' services, organising them institutionally in terms that depend on public provision rather than markets.[7]

There are many problems with this approach.[8] The field is littered with 'black swans' – exceptions to the confident generalisations that régime analysis depends on. Australia is not 'liberal' in the sense of restricting social intervention, but 'radically redistributive'.[9] If Britain is 'liberal', the universal health service does not fit the mould. France is not just a cross between other systems; it has a distinctive model in its own right.[10] Several writers have tried to expand the number of models to take into account the bewildering number of exceptions. The attempt is doomed to failure; there are simply too many variations to be fitted into the boxes available. Welfare systems are not a unified whole: 'welfare' is a catch-all term that may or may not include education, pensions or, depending on whether it is done publicly or privately, health care. Talking about 'welfare states' is no reason to suppose that the same principles will apply across all these fields at the same time.[11] The neat categorisations collapse when the reality is examined: "the devil is in the detail."[12]

It is probably more helpful to think of welfare states in terms of their 'family resemblance'. In a family, there are often strong likenesses, but people can resemble each other in different ways, and the more distant relatives may not resemble each other directly at all. The United Kingdom is more like Sweden when it emphasises rights to health care and more like Australia when it deals with unemployment. France is more like Germany when it emphasises occupational status and more like Spain in its handling of education. And once we are resigned to think of welfare states as a broad cluster of approaches, it becomes possible to think in general terms about some of the characteristics that welfare states share.

These characteristics are not really what might be expected from the label of the welfare state, because they are not necessarily about the 'state' at all. The assumption made in many discussions is that the provision of welfare is the

---

7. G. Esping-Andersen, 1990, The three worlds of welfare capitalism, Cambridge: Polity.

8. P. Spicker, 1996, Normative comparisons of social security systems, in L. Hantrais and S. Mangen (eds.), Cross-national research methods in the social sciences, London: Pinter.

9. B. Cass and J. Freeland, 1994, Social Security and full employment in Australia, in J. Hills, J. Ditch and H. Glennerster (eds.), Beveridge and social security, Oxford: Clarendon Press.

10. P. Spicker, 2002, France, in J. Dixon and R. Scheurell (eds.), The state of social welfare: the twentieth century in cross-national review, Westport, CT: Praeger, pp. 109–24.

11. See F. Castles, 2008, What welfare states do, Journal of Social Policy 38(1), 45–62.

12. J. Ditch, 1999, Full circle: a second coming for social assistance? in J. Clasen (ed.), Comparative social policy, Oxford: Blackwell.

same thing as provision by government. In most countries, that is just not true. The normal pattern of welfare provision is a 'mixed economy', in which welfare is delivered through a combination of government, independent non-profit and mutualist services. The European welfare states depended heavily on the services provided by employers, trades unions and voluntary associations, and in many cases the 'state' came late to the party. The welfare states are characterised, first, by the processes that have led to the establishment of systems of mutual support; second, by the complexity of the range of supportive networks and the interplay among them; and third, by the issues and problems faced by governments in adapting to such systems. Social policy is a combination of policies, practices and institutional approaches developed by a wide range of actors, not only by government; and a welfare state is not so much a pattern of government provision as a complex set of social arrangements – a welfare system.

WHAT WELFARE STATES DO

Although there is no single model of the welfare state, there are some recurring themes: that welfare provision is intended to meet people's needs, that it should offer social protection or that it should serve some other kinds of social purpose. The kinds of needs that are commonly met in welfare states include

- low income, especially through the interruption of earnings
- social care for older people and those with disabilities
- education for children, and sometimes for young adults
- medical care, primarily of the kind given in hospitals (provision for primary care and medical goods is more uneven), and
- provisions relating to public health, including drainage, sanitation and basic housing quality.

It is possible to see these as providing for 'essentials', but if so there is some arbitrariness in defining what is essential and what is not. The list does not include basic items like food, clothing or fuel – it tends to assume that if people need those things, they will be able to buy them. There are other things which are vitally important to people but have little to do with welfare provision – for example, love, friendship and emotional support. The activities are best understood as the product of conventional practice and policy transfer; countries have learned from each other what is expected.

There are some common understandings of problems across welfare states – retirement in old age is commonplace, and a lot of work has been done to arrive at international definitions of 'unemployment' – but other terms like 'family policy', exclusion, disability or homelessness mean different things in different places. It is broadly true that the largest and most important group identified in most welfare states consists of older people, usually defined on the basis of a retirement age in the mid- to late sixties. The key elements of support are pensions, health care and support for disability in old age. Depending on the size of the elderly population, most welfare states spend well over half, and something up to two-thirds, of their budgets in supporting this group. The next largest group covers younger people with disabilities, long-term physical illness and incapacity for work (though such conditions are again skewed to older adults within that group, reflecting the importance of disabling conditions like stroke). This generalisation is not as safe as the first. Though the circumstances are different – people with disabilities can work, people with incapacities may be ill rather than disabled – some countries do not make any effective distinction between disability and incapacity for work: that usually means that people who really should be supported in one way have to apply for support under the other category if they are to get any help.

Some welfare states have explicit family policies and some do not, but most have policies that are about families, so it makes some sense to treat this as the next main contingency. Family policy, usually understood as support for parents with younger children, is partly financial, partly related to education, partly the promotion of health and partly the protection of vulnerable children. And then there is a general set of problems relating to low or interrupted income, often identified with 'poverty', though poverty is a much broader concept. Low incomes may be a marker for a range of other problems, including disability, unemployment and educational disadvantage, but – despite the common stereotypes of long-term poverty and inter-generational deprivation – most people on low incomes in developed countries do not stay in that condition indefinitely. The effect of changes in the economic environment, education and new household formation leads many people to move to higher incomes, while unemployment, divorce and disability lead other people to move to lower ones. But low income matters, because it directly affects access to essential goods like food and fuel, decent housing and services like transport and communications.

Some welfare states provide some services universally as a right for all citizens; examples are universal basic education and essential health care. Other services are provided on a residual, 'safety net' basis for those who are unable to get the service by other means. Most welfare states have some form of social assistance, offering income-related benefits and services, but the provisions made by most developed welfare states are concerned not so much with direct responses to need as with situations in which needs might otherwise arise, such as old age, unemployment and disability.

Some services are uniform, provided to large numbers of people or communities: roads, schools or public health. Others are more personalised, adapted to the needs of the individual: medical care, social work or cash assistance. One of the central issues identified by Esping-Andersen is the question of 'decommodification' – the extent to which the supply of certain goods and services are taken outside the economic market and provided directly. This is not a choice between supporting people and not supporting them; it is more commonly a question of whether assistance should be provided in terms of money to spend (which is how food and clothing are usually distributed) or goods and services to use (the main way that basic education is provided in the welfare states, an option for health care and affordable housing).

WELFARE SPENDING: HOW DISCUSSIONS ABOUT WELFARE GO ASTRAY

Discussions about the welfare state tend to go astray when they focus on 'welfare' as a big, undifferentiated, unitary concept. Many debates about welfare centre on public expenditure. Take this example, attributed to Angela Merkel, the German Chancellor and currently the most powerful politician in Europe: that the European Union (EU) accounts for 7 percent of the world's population, 25 percent of its GDP, and 50 percent of its welfare spending.[13] The implication is that European spending on welfare is excessive. Her figures are wrong – Europe actually accounts for about 40 percent of world 'expenditure' in these terms[14] – but that is not the main objection. By comparing European expenditure to the rest of the world, Merkel is implicitly comparing Germany and France to the likes of Somalia and the Congo. Unsurprisingly welfare in those countries is not given the same priority that it is in Europe – they have other problems, and much more limited resources to deal with them. Rich countries spend proportionately more on welfare than poor countries for a very simple reason: they are the ones who have the money to spend. Figure 1.1 shows that a relationship is discernible between spending and national income in the richest countries, the members of the OECD (the Organisation for Economic Cooperation and Development).[15]

Within those figures, one driver is particularly prominent: spending on older people. Expenditure on older people – typically for pensions, social

---

13. Economist, 2013, The Merkel plan, June 5.
14. I. Begg, F. Mushovel and R. Niblett, 2015, The welfare state in Europe, London: Chatham House, p. 4.
15. Data from OECD, 2016, OECD.stat, http://stats.oecd.org/.

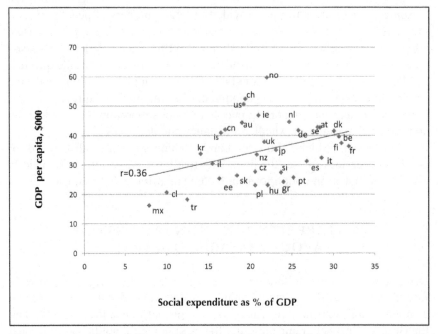

Figure 1.1.   Social expenditure in richer countries rises with income per capita.

care, health care and social assistance – is one of the characteristic features of contemporary welfare states. Figure 1.2 shows that the richer a country becomes, the more it is likely to spend on older people. This pattern is surprisingly uncontroversial – some people have argued that welfare states cannot afford to support elderly people, but very few are prepared to argue directly that it's a bad thing to do. Making that case is, however, implicit in any general argument that providing welfare is too costly.

Any general observation about the welfare state which is based on this kind of evidence has to be treated with caution. There are other factors determining social expenditure, and in any case expenditure is not the same thing as social welfare provision.[16]   Then, at this level of generality, it is not really possible to tell how much will be spent on what kind of activity. There is a weak association between the treatment of pensioners, people with disabilities, unemployed people and children – countries which spend more on one tend to spend more on another simply because they're countries that spend

---

16. Castles, 2008, 45–62.

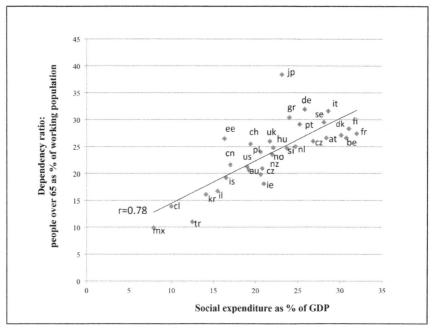

Figure 1.2. Social spending rises with the number of older people.

more – but that's about as far as it goes. The links are not particularly clear or strong. Like many observations in this field, the evidence relies on small numbers of cases and the interpretation can be distorted through biased selection or missing data.

This point is difficult to demonstrate using published studies, because much of the distortion that results is invisible. When social scientists prepare analyses on the basis of international comparisons, they try to plug the gaps – finding information that is comparable, ensuring conformity with the statistical assumptions and trying to avoid the traps. It is difficult for the general reader to identify the choices that have been made and understand the consequences – it is rare enough for the information even to be provided to the peer reviewers who are supposed to safeguard the quality of published research. There is no way of knowing what alternative analyses might have shown, and unless readers repeat the work for themselves they cannot hope to know what effect the process of sorting and sifting has had on the results.

Figure 1.3 offers a cautionary example. Many critics of welfare provision find it plausible to suppose that welfare leads people not to work. The figure is drawn,

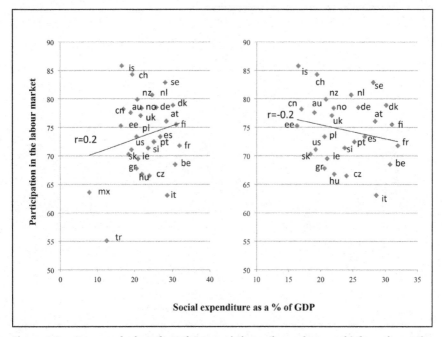

Figure 1.3.   Two graphs based on the same information: what we think we know depends on the data we choose.

like the others, from indicators produced by the OECD for 2014.[17] It seems to show the relationship between social expenditure and labour market participation. The poorest countries tend to have low labour market participation, because people have to manage outside the formal economy; middle income countries generally have more, but there are likely to be excluded groups and women may find it more difficult to work. In general terms, richer countries tend to have higher rates of participation in the labour market. The same richer countries tend to spend more on welfare, so insofar as we can tell what effect welfare has, we can at least say that it doesn't seem to be associated with dependency.

The evidence is inconclusive, however, and the two charts in the figure help to explain why. I have not altered the data directly – it is common practice in comparative analysis to look for the best fit possible, transforming data mathematically to make the relationships clearer – but I have made some choices, including the choices of the specific example. One of the conventions of statistical analysis is to eliminate outliers, because aberrant individual results can distort other results. For example, Luxembourg has been omitted from all the charts as an outlier – its population is very small and its very high average

---

17. Data from OECD, 2016.

income excludes many people in a workforce that travels from neighbouring countries. The two graphs based on the rest of the data are almost identical – if they look slightly different, it is mainly because the axis for the graph on the right is shorter. The key difference is that the graph on the left contains data for Turkey and Mexico and the graph on the right does not. The effect of that small change in the selection of data is sufficient to reverse the direction of the apparent relationship. That is already a warning that the evidence can be crucially influenced by the selection of countries – but it is not the whole story. What the graphs do not show is as important as what they do. Some information is missing from both charts – gaps in data are, unfortunately, common, and at the time I put the chart together, data were not available for Japan, Korea and Chile. Korea's figures were published subsequently: labour market participation and social expenditure are both lower than Turkey's. That makes it more difficult to justify treating Turkey and Mexico as outliers, unless there is also a case for considering Korea an outlier too.

The main weaknesses in comparative analysis at this level are methodological rather than evidential. Welfare states have some common characteristics, but they are also highly diverse. There is no single set of arrangements to be assessed. The links are complex and multifaceted, and the evidence is always equivocal. It is always difficult to exclude alternative explanations. Generalised studies of the impact of unemployment benefits, for example, mean very little if they cannot control for the differences in the economic, social and administrative context where they occur. Even if there is good reason to suppose that social phenomena are linked – for example, that women have fewer children when infant mortality falls, or that labour market participation tends to be higher in richer countries – it is not self-evident that social welfare provision is what makes a difference. The process of comparison simply cannot deliver the certainty about effects that policy makers would like to have.

A lengthy review of similar evidence would serve little purpose other than to show that it cannot support the sort of confident generalisations that are usually made in debates about welfare. Most statements of supposed fact, both for and against the welfare state, are open to question. However, the reservations that social scientists learn to express are not often reflected in political debates. People see in the evidence what they expect to see. Most of us are liable to 'confirmation bias';[18] we select evidence, look for findings that reinforce our prejudices and apply greater critical tests to the points we disagree with than the ones we do.

There is a more fundamental problem lurking underneath these arguments. There are constant complaints that spending on welfare is a drain on the

18. R. Nickerson, 1998, Confirmation bias, Review of General Psychology 2(2), 175–220.

economy, that it promotes dependency and that it pushes states into financial crisis; but there is no consistent relationship between welfare spending and economic performance,[19] the argument that it promotes dependency runs counter to such evidence as there is, and the welfare states haven't collapsed. It hardly seems to matter what the evidence shows – political argument does not depend on it. The assertion that welfare is unaffordable is really about whether welfare should be afforded. Criticisms of dependency challenge whether some people should be able to have an income paid for by other people's contributions. Predictions of doom are used to challenge whether current commitments should continue to exist. That is why the critics continually come back to these positions regardless of what the evidence shows. This is not really a debate about evidence; it is about ideas and moral principles. This book is a defence of the welfare state. Its main purpose is to set out the normative basis for welfare provision – to say why welfare ought to be provided – rather than reviewing evidence as to what happens when it is.

---

19. A. B. Atkinson, 1995, The welfare state and economic performance, in Incomes and the welfare state, Cambridge: Cambridge University Press, ch. 6.

Chapter Two

The Moral Basis of Social Policy

The most basic argument for welfare provision lies in the conviction that it is the right thing to do. The most basic arguments against welfare are, equally, moral – a belief that providing welfare is wrong.

Morals are norms which govern conduct. Most moral norms are concerned with social conduct, though not all are, and some of those relate to people's welfare. Deciding whether an action is 'good' or 'right' cannot be done simply by looking at the way things are, and ethical positions have to be understood according to ethical criteria. Ethical positions typically boil down to one of four positions:

- that moral behaviour has good consequences,
- that moral rules are universal – intrinsically right and applicable to everyone,
- that morality depends on a fabric of particular obligations, which are individual and specific to every person, or
- that moral actions are characteristic of moral conduct and can be said to stem from 'virtues'.

CONSEQUENCES

There are some moral principles which value an action according to the consequences. These are referred to as consequentialist or teleological theories, and they are based on the view that well-being is good in itself. Consequentialism can be taken to support the provision of welfare – this is almost circular, because well-being is what good actions are supposed to produce. The main way that this is liable to be opposed is through an argument that the provision of welfare, regardless of good intentions, has bad or undesirable consequences.

The best known teleological theory is utilitarianism. The eighteenth-century philosopher Jeremy Bentham was in his day the most influential writer on social policy. He argued that the action which was best morally was the one which increased welfare (or 'utility') to the greatest degree at the least cost.[1] In other words, the most moral action is the one which has the best consequences, and Bentham took this to be about 'the greatest happiness of the greatest number'. This is not equivalent to saying that all actions which increase an individual's welfare are good – because there are costs to be considered, and because there are other ways in which consequences must be judged besides the viewpoint of a single person – but it does mean that it is a good thing to increase well-being when other things are equal. Bentham's principles have been built in to modern-day economics. Cost/benefit analysis (CBA) works by calculating who is going to benefit and who is going to pay, and if there is more benefit than cost, the thing can get done. That is rather tough on the people who carry the costs – the people whose houses get knocked down to make way for roads or shopping centres, the ones who are put at risk of flooding to reduce the risk to others, the unfortunate residents who have to put up with the noise of aeroplanes so that others can travel. The main defence of CBA is that at least it makes it clear who wins and who loses; the main problem is that what some people gain does not justify what others lose.

Bentham's approach is based on a judgement about individual actions and is known as 'act-utilitarianism'. John Stuart Mill's modified version of utilitarianism is based on rules and is known as 'rule-utilitarianism'. Mill argued that moral actions were those which overall are most likely to lead to good consequences and, conversely, that an action is immoral if "the action is of a class which, if practised generally, would be generally injurious."[2] Education is generally compulsory, because education is generally beneficial and permitting exceptions would generally be harmful. Medical services hold in general to a principle of confidentiality, because reporting problems in some spheres may lead to people being reluctant to report ill health. Rules should be upheld, Mill argued, even if they were damaging in particular cases.

Rule-utilitarianism is superficially appealing, but it is difficult to hold to: if a rule is justified because it yields a good result in most cases, is that a good enough reason to apply it in those cases in which its effects are not good? The

---

1. J. Bentham, 1789, An introduction to the principles of morals and legislation, in M. Warnock (ed.), Utilitarianism, Glasgow: Collins, 1962.

2. J. S. Mill, 1861, Utilitarianism, in M. Warnock (ed.), Utilitarianism, Glasgow: Collins, 1962, p. 270.

actions of most constitutional governments are bound by a system of rules: such governments can do what they are permitted by their constitution and no more. That has led in the United States to the federal government hesitating about intervention in the case of natural disaster. (Questions about the powers of government are considered further in chapter 7.)

It has been argued that the pursuit of welfare is necessarily consequentialist – and so that social policy must of necessity be utilitarian or something very like it. This is questionable. It may be the pursuit of welfare, rather than its achievement, which is valued morally, because of what it says about the morality of a society and the people in it. It is no less possible that the pursuit of welfare may be seen as an expression of moral values, rather than a supreme value in itself. If 'humanitarianism', 'brotherly love' or 'grace' are seen as moral ideals, individual or collective action may be seen as the consequences of these principles, rather than as principles in themselves. Besides, welfare may be only one value of many.

UNIVERSAL PRINCIPLES

Moral theories which see certain values as intrinsically right – right in themselves – are usually referred to as deontological or duty-based. Deontological principles imply moral obligations, typically expressed in terms of principles or moral rules. They take the form of prohibitions (describing things that should not be done) or prescriptions (things that ought to be done).

Some views of morality are absolute – universal and applying to all societies at all times. Religious principles might well be universal. Several religions – not all! – believe that their moral codes are ordained by God for everyone, and moral rules governing, for example, sexuality, suicide, abortion or charity have strong religious foundations. Most of the world's great religions have something to say about charity and responsibility to other human beings. The Bible tells us that

> If there be among you a needy man, one of thy brethren, within any of thy gates, in thy land which the Lord thy God giveth thee, thou shalt not harden thy heart, nor shut thy hand from thy needy brother; but thou shalt surely open thy hand unto him, and shalt surely lend him sufficient for his need in that which he wanteth.[3]

Mediaeval Christianity took the principle of charity to be a duty to God, not to the poor person; that approach has largely been superseded in Christianity

---

3. Deuteronomy 15:7–8.

with the modern emphases on individualism, liberation (which emphasises the importance of social justice) and solidarity. Islam has a general duty to give charity, zakat, which is linked to social justice as well as to religious duties.[4] The Buddha once travelled to give instruction to a poor man, but he made sure he was fed first.

However, focusing solely on the words of scriptures or prophets does not really convey what the religion is teaching. In part, that happens because simple phrases can be read in different ways. If the poor are blessed, will they still be blessed if they are helped to avoid poverty? There are some religious authorities who might argue that whatever happens to be true ought to be left alone – that charity does not address the things that are important spiritually, that social attempts to change the order of things defy God's will. Where humanitarianism says that 'something must be done', this kind of religious conservatism says that nothing should be. The key word in that description is not religion, but conservatism, because it is hard to think of any religious doctrine which could not equally refer to a countervailing principle.

There have been many attempts to give universal morality a foundation in reason and argument. It is possible to make a case for some universal principles on the basis of consistency. If people are being dealt with morally, the argument runs, then people in like circumstances should be responded to by the same criteria, without the sense of arbitrariness, unfairness or privilege that inconsistency implies. Immanuel Kant suggested that any legitimate morality should be generalisable: "Act only on that maxim through which you can at the same time will that it should become a universal law."[5] A moral action has to be based in rules, and the rules must apply to everyone, not just to one particular case. A further proposition is that one should act 'as if you were through your maxims a law-making member of a kingdom of ends.' It means that each person must treat his or her rules seriously and be bound by the rules which are applied.

Possibly the most influential expression of this kind of universalism in the contemporary world is the idea of human rights. Human rights depend on a claim that common rules apply to everyone by virtue of their humanity. Traditionally, the argument for common standards has taken the form of a reference to 'natural law'. For Thomas Aquinas, the Catholic theologian, "Rational creatures have a certain share in the divine reason itself. . . . This participation in the eternal law by rational creatures is called the natural law."[6] The fusion of natural and divine law leads to views that what is natural

---

4. S. Kotb, 1970, Social justice in Islam, New York: Octagon Books.
5. H. Paton, 1948, The moral law: Kant's groundwork of the metaphysics of morals, London: Hutchinson, p. 84.
6. A. d'Entrèves, 1970, Natural law, London: Hutchinson, p. 43.

is both right and in accord with God's design – like childbirth, the responsibilities of parents and even (though this may also be thought to be socially determined) the possession of property.

Ultimately, none of this is really susceptible to argument – one accepts the case for universal principles or one does not. There have been people who reject such ideas altogether – Jeremy Bentham famously dismissed claims to natural rights as "nonsense on stilts" – but it is more common to find that critics accept some universal rights (typically rights to life, liberty and property) while rejecting others. The Universal Declaration of Human Rights stakes a claim for "a standard of living adequate for the health and well-being of [the person] and his family, including food, clothing, housing and medical care and necessary social services."[7] The UN's *Guiding Principles on Extreme Poverty and Human Rights* flesh out the details, including issues such as stigmatisation, access to justice and the denial of basic liberties to the dispossessed.[8]

PARTICULAR OBLIGATIONS

Many of the moral principles that guide people are consistent, but they are not universal – they do not apply to everyone. When one person makes a promise to another or agrees to a contract, there is an obligation, but the obligation only applies between those two people. This is a 'particular' obligation, rather than a general one.

Particular moral norms are norms which affect the relationships between people in specified relationships – for example, the norms that shape how family members relate to each other, whether promises are kept, or what happens in a marriage. This kind of obligation is central to many systems of welfare provision. There are some entitlements based on nationality or residence, which are fairly general criteria, but other entitlements to services tend to be personalised – they typically depend on issues like contributions and work record. Pensions in continental Europe are routinely delivered on the basis of earned entitlement; provision for unemployment varies, but parts of it work on a similar principle. These are examples of particular rights, rather than universal ones. Particular rights are rights which are specific to a particular person in a particular time and place. Contractual rights are an example, and pensions are often delivered through contracts.

When religious principles were mentioned before, it was to describe teachings which might be taken to apply to everyone. What most religions

---

7. United Nations, 1948, Universal declaration of human rights, Article 25(1).
8. United Nations, 2012, Guiding principles on extreme poverty and human rights, Geneva: Office of the High Commissioner for Human Rights.

have in common, however, is not so much a sense of universal obligation to fellow humans as of specific communal obligations. Religion, regardless of the formal content of teachings, is more than a moral voice; it is the organising force behind a complex network of solidaristic, voluntary and charitable networks. It is in this light that religious arguments have to be understood. Many religious institutions are founded on a communal basis. In Judaism, the Talmud makes specific recommendations for communal organisation and administration of charity.[9] In Christianity, the Church asserted both its right and its obligation to oversee and safeguard the operation of charity;[10] during the Reformation, similar arguments were turned against the Church itself, with an insistence that this oversight should be managed through civic authority, and many countries have developed a complex mix of secular and religious provision. The Quran identifies several groups that require assistance: the destitute, those in need, people overwhelmed by debt and those who are subject to natural disasters. The major charitable institutions are the waqfs, non-profit organisations which can exist in perpetuity.[11]

If religion is a form of social organisation, a secular state might supplant it. There may then be resistance to the idea that the state should do things which fall in the sphere of the religious authorities. This is not intrinsic to religious views, but it can be very influential. Some religions, and some countries, have made a firm distinction between the secular and religious spheres of their societies – there are examples in France (predominantly Catholic) and the United States (no longer predominantly Protestant, but certainly Christian). Others have established religions and churches, including the formally Christian United Kingdom, the Jewish state of Israel or the Islamic Republics of Iran or Pakistan. Some religious groups are radical, arguing for fundamental political and social change; others are conservative, arguing either for support for established regimes or at least acceptance of the status quo.

The emphasis on particular moral norms is sometimes described in terms of a 'communitarian' perspective. Universal principles apply to everyone; communitarianism, by contrast, states that each person has special responsibilities to some others (such as family members), and that our moral duties define how close we are to those people. There is no necessary inconsistency between universalism and communitarianism, which can be held to at the same time, but different balances imply different social policies. Communitarians argue that rights, norms, principles and moral action cannot sensibly be understood

---

9. Talmud, Tractate Baba Bathra.

10. J. Brodman, 2009, Charity and religion in medieval Europe, Washington, DC: Catholic University of America Press.

11. S. Heyneman (ed.), 2004, Islam and social policy, Nashville: Vanderbilt University Press.

in universal terms; everyone is born into a network of social relationships, and morals have to be understood in the context in which they are applied.

Communitarian thinking seems to support the idea of a welfare state – a society in which people accept responsibility for each other and develop ways of protecting their fellows. That can be construed to support the idea of a welfare state, but at the same time, it poses a difficult challenge for it. Bill Jordan argues that the same processes which protect people – citizenship, pension schemes and social assistance – also generate social exclusion for others.[12] In a society which is diverse, the bonds that hold different groups together may be less important than the bonds which distinguish them. So the relatively monocultural countries of Northern Europe have been model welfare states with a universalist ethos; the United States, a vibrant, multicultural society, has 'decentralized social altruism'[13] – a rich patchwork of provision at local or community level – but limits the size and scope of its commitment to welfare. Other countries with an active tradition of admitting immigrants – Australia, Canada and Israel – are categorised by Esping-Andersen as 'liberal' regimes, on the basis that they tend to interpret entitlements restrictively. As European countries become more diverse culturally, there is a risk that they may go the same way, with people confining their altruism to those who are most like themselves.

VIRTUE ETHICS

A fourth class of moral arguments is very old, but has only relatively recently begun to feature prominently in academic writing on ethics. This is 'virtue ethics', a line of argument derived from Aristotle. Aristotle argued that a good action was an action of the sort that a good person would do. A virtuous action is not guided by the principle or by its consequences, but by the type of person who does it.[14] The idea has been revived in modern writing, for example by MacIntyre,[15] who fuses the idea with elements of communitarianism.

The emphasis on virtue rather than principle does not seem to fit most of the ideas which have been considered, and at first sight it may not make a great deal of sense; morality is about much more than character. The power of the argument is clearest in relation to children: most parents do not raise their children to do the right thing in every case, but to be a good person. Trying

---

12. B. Jordan, 1996, A theory of poverty and social exclusion, Brighton: Polity.
13. G. Klass, 1985, Explaining America and the welfare state, British Journal of Political Science 15, 427–50.
14. Aristotle, Nichomachean Ethics, Book 2, in J. Thomson (ed.), 1953, The ethics of Aristotle, Harmondsworth: Penguin.
15. A. MacIntyre, 1981, After virtue, London: Duckworth.

to tell children what is the right thing is virtually impossible; no-one can possible anticipate all the circumstances. But it is possible to show children how to react and what kind of sentiments they should have, and moral conduct follows from those. Parents try to teach children to be honest, considerate, well-mannered and so forth. These are 'virtues', and that is why this approach to morality is called 'virtue ethics'.

Virtue ethics can be taken to justify both moral duties to support welfare and opposition to it, because the assessment of virtue depends on the values that are attached to it. On one hand, we may wish people, government and society to be considerate, generous, humanitarian and mutually supportive; on the other, we may prize the virtues of independence, self-determination and self-help, which have all been used to resist the idea that welfare should be publicly provided. There may also be a view of what makes for virtuous government and what a government should or should not do: government should strive, among other things, to be democratic, representative, just, deliberative and effective. Views about the legitimacy of government action play an important part in resistance to the idea of public provision.

MORALITY AND WELFARE

There is no easy way to choose between these four positions, and most of us hop back and forth between them at different times, depending on the context and the reason for the argument. For practical purposes, however, a principled view probably offers the clearest statements of what is right and wrong, and much of what follows is based in principles.

The moral grounds for providing social welfare services are easily stated. In terms of the consequences, welfare has good consequences for the person who receives it. No-one out there really wants to argue for the abolition of pensions. Nearly every developed society has made arrangements for people to receive health care, and most of the richest societies have sought to do this fairly generally for their populations. The United States stands out as an exception, but even in that case there are some striking examples of communal provision – Medicare for older people, the provision made by state governments (the schemes in Hawaii and Minnesota are particularly noteworthy) and a Veterans Administration that protects millions of veterans and their families on the basis that the community owes something back.[16] In terms of principles, there are few systems of morality that would not think it appro-

---

16. A. Kovner and J. Knickman, 2013, Jonas and Kovner's health care delivery in the United States, New York: Springer.

priate to feed the hungry, clothe the naked, help the sick and so forth. That is a common humanitarian impulse, and the expansion of the issues into the language of human rights is only a stronger expression of that impulse. In terms of virtue, charity and altruism are generally considered emblematic of virtue. A society in which people help each other is a better society than one in which people don't.

The moral arguments against welfare have, then, some obstacles to overcome. They do it typically in three main ways. If the focus is consequentialist, the main approach is to argue that welfare has negative consequences – for example, that it leads to dependency or undermines the people it is supposed to support. If morality is formed in terms of general principles, the main way of addressing the moral imperatives is either to claim that they are irrelevant (the position, for example, of Robert Nozick, who opposes all 'patterned' forms of redistribution),[17] that they override other, more valuable principles (such as freedom or property ownership) or that there are other moral factors at work – the immorality or the irresponsibility of people who receive welfare – which excuse the initial sense of moral responsibility that caring people might otherwise feel. If morality is about virtue, the principal objection to welfare is that it undermines the virtue of its recipients – encouraging them, for example, to have children out of wedlock, to flout social conventions or to engage in antisocial behaviour.

There are some common themes here. The critics of welfare often want to claim that welfare has bad effects, that it is immoral or that it leads to bad people – sometimes, for example in the work of Charles Murray[18] or Lawrence Mead,[19] all three at once. For the most part, those criticisms are morally irrelevant. Saying that welfare is difficult or that some people misbehave, even if it makes some people feel they can wash their hands of the issue, does not make moral responsibilities disappear.

There is not much in these objections, either, to counter communitarian arguments. On occasion one hears alarm and despondency about the unsustainable undertakings that have been made to pensioners – that is a consequentialist position – but on the whole it is unusual to hear principled moral objections to the idea that people have some earned rights, and more unusual still for the extent to which welfare provision in developed countries depends on such rights to be recognised in such critiques. It is convenient for those who oppose 'welfare' to suppose that it is the product of overweening government and that those who are engaged in it are the victims of compulsion

---

17. R. Nozick, 1974, Anarchy, state and utopia, Oxford: Blackwell.
18. C. Murray, 1984, Losing ground, New York: Basic Books.
19. L. Mead, 1992, The new politics of poverty, New York: Basic Books.

against their interests. That is far from the experience of many welfare states in the world, where welfare systems have developed on a voluntary basis and governments have stepped in only belatedly.[20]

THE MAIN ARGUMENTS FOR WELFARE IN CHAPTER 2

Welfare is the right thing to do if

- it has good consequences,

- it is consistent with general moral rules, such as human rights or the principles of major religions,

- it is done in recognition of specific obligations or

- it is the sort of thing done by good people.

---

20. P. Baldwin, 1990, The politics of social solidarity, Cambridge: Cambridge University Press.

Chapter Three

Benefitting Other People

Some arguments for welfare are altruistic: the proposition that it is good for one person to do things to benefit other people, even if those other people are strangers. If people do each other good, that is mutual, and the arrangement can be described as a form of exchange.

The idea of altruism conflates several other concepts, including moral duties to other people. It may be possible to distinguish, among others,

- moral duty – adherence to a moral code that instructs people to consider others, or acceptance that altruism is virtuous because providing for others is what a good person would do;
- benevolence and kindness – wishing good for other people and doing it;
- humanitarianism – justification of moral conduct in terms of common humanity or sympathy;
- reciprocity – a return for past favours, anticipation of future favours or a sense that people should give back something for what they receive; and
- 'pro-social' behaviour – the term is used in social psychology to refer not just to benevolent action, but to the everyday round of behaviour, interaction, exchange and cooperation in which people help others.

Altruism is often seen as a 'pure' ideal, in which considerations of the benefit of other people are not mixed with other issues such as the benefit to the giver. When Richard Titmuss wrote about altruism in *The Gift Relationship*,[1] it provoked a hostile reaction from some critics on the 'New Right', who argued there

---

1. R. M. Titmuss, 1970, The gift relationship, Harmondsworth: Penguin.

was no such thing as 'pure' altruism, and that whenever people give to others they get something back, such as a sense of worth, status or satisfaction.[2] That may or may not be true, but it is not relevant: Titmuss based his arguments not on pure altruism but on 'gift-exchange', treating the two issues almost as equivalent. Altruism means only that people do something for the good of other people.

Benevolence is partly about disposition – wishing good for other people – and partly about action – doing good things. Benevolence tends, in its nature, to be personal and immediate rather than generalised, so it fits better with a communitarian model than with universalist principles. Humanitarian actions are done for the benefit of other human beings (usually understood to be 'other' in the sense that they extend beyond a person's own family). Adam Smith saw the origin of such actions in the sympathy or fellow-feeling that people experience when they see another person in distress.[3] Some of the critics of social welfare provision have suggested that formal organisation, and particularly organisation by the state, could tend to drive out personal benevolence;[4] and Titmuss's arguments suggest that the need to give has to be respected in a society, not just the need to receive. Nevertheless, there is probably a sense in which the extension of welfare can be attributed to benevolence in a more general sense; many of the arguments of early reformers were seen as an extension of the principle of charity, a means to social reform or a way of redeeming the poor.

Humanitarianism is a broader, more universal version of benevolence. The appeal to common humanity is too wide to be of much use; it is hardly possible for humanitarians to care about everyone. It is difficult to see how humanitarians could accept the position in which other people are starved, oppressed or enslaved. For much of human history, however, that is just what good people have done. Most of us manage to get through the day without even thinking about the position of people living in poverty in Burkina Faso. Part of the human condition is that we spend rather more time thinking about people who are closer to us and less time about those who are distant; that is how we know they are closer. That does not mean that humanitarianism is impossible, but it does mean that benevolence tends to be particular, rather than universal.

There are limits as to how far an understanding of altruistic action can take us in the analysis of welfare. It is not evident that altruistic conduct will lead immediately or directly to any of the forms of social organisation associated with social welfare. In certain cases – notably the Reformation, in which city burghers may have wanted to restrict the exercise of charity by religious orders,[5] and the plea of 'scientific' charity in the nineteenth century not to let

---

2. M. Cooper and A. Culyer, 1968, The price of blood, London: Institute of Economic Affairs.
3. A. Smith, 1759, The theory of moral sentiments.
4. For example, D. Green, 1993, Reinventing civil society, London: Civitas.
5. See P. Spicker, 2010, The origins of modern welfare, Oxford: Peter Lang.

kindness encourage the growth of a dependent population[6] – the organisation of welfare has developed to restrict the exercise of private charity. It is not obvious, either, that people's altruism can or should be mobilised into any agreement for governments to provide welfare, as opposed to any other way of doing things. However, they can come to think that 'something must be done', and the history of several welfare states has been that social provision has gradually expanded as governments and mutual aid societies have tried to respond to urgent and pressing moral claims. This is a haphazard and sometimes irrational process. Once welfare systems are in place, altruism offers a justification for the things that the systems do.

It is difficult to argue against humanitarianism, partly because it is vague, but also because it is difficult to make a virtue of selfishness. Herbert Spencer thought that the "survival of the fittest" would lead to a better society[7] – his expression was later borrowed by Darwin for other purposes – and there are contemporary writers who argue for systems entirely based on the power of individual self-interest, but the basis of their argument is usually that those arrangements will lead to greater well-being, not that there is no scope for humanitarian action. If altruism is learned in childhood, however, so are the arguments against it. In the much-loved children's story, the little red hen asks for help to plant wheat, grow it and tend it, but she does not get it.

> "Who will help me cut the wheat?"
> "Not I," barked the dog.
> "Not I," purred the cat.
> "Not I," quacked the duck
> "Then I will," said the little red hen.

So when it comes to eating the bread, she eats it herself and does not share. The story is even more delightful when accompanied by colourful pictures and animal noises. There are two common themes here. One is the view that people own and control the things they work for. The other is the idea that those who don't work don't get – also expressed in the dictum of St Paul, that "if a man does not work, nor shall he eat". There is quite a gap between taking that as a description and treating it as a prescription of how people ought to be treated.

The *Little Red Hen* represents a powerful series of myths, reflected for example in the work of Henry Thoreau in the nineteenth century or Robert Nozick in the twentieth. It reflects the image of self-sufficient farmers, the pioneer on the American frontier or the apocalyptic fantasies of Hollywood.

---

6. K. Woodroofe, 1966, From charity to social work, London: Routledge and Kegan Paul, ch. 2.
7. H. Spencer, 1864, Man versus the state.

None of us is self-sufficient or ever will be. People are born into families and communities. The food we eat, the clothes we wear, the buildings we live in, the water we drink and the tools we use are the products of social interaction and exchange. People who think that something is all their own work are usually under a misapprehension.

SOCIAL RESPONSIBILITY

Margaret Thatcher famously claimed that there is no such thing as society.[8] There are apologists who claim that she didn't really mean that, but the position is well established in the literature about individualism and freedom: some extreme individualists, like Bentham, do not recognise the existence of any collective entity.[9] In the most individualistic models of society, the position of each person is a product of a range of factors; each person has 'agency', the power to make decisions and exercise control over outcomes, and generalisations about social position cannot be made consistently. Even within that very limited understanding of society, however, there are relationships between people that are about more than government on one hand and the individual on the other – relationships, among others, of family, community, voluntary associations, occupation, religion and ethnicity. Many people identify themselves with particular social groups; they may have many overlapping identities.

It is fairly easy to see why a business, a university or a church is something different from the sum of the individual people who make it up. A 'society', however, is not quite like any of those examples. For Oakeshott, the term was a shapeless concept, assuming some kind of association without saying what the association might be.[10] There is some justification for that, because there is a lot of lazy thinking about society – treating society as an area ruled over by a government, people who happen to be in one place, another word for 'everybody'. Society is much more than any of those things. Human beings are social animals. They are part of families, communities and cultures. Every person is born and raised within a complex, overlapping set of relationships: identity, ownership, history and culture matter. Identities, relationships and responsibilities shift, but people are part of networks and groups in which

---

8. M. Thatcher, 1987, Interview for Women's Own, http://www.margaretthatcher.org/document/106689.

9. J. Bentham, 1789, An introduction to the principles of morals and legislation, in M. Warnock (ed.), Utilitarianism, Glasgow: Collins, 1962.

10. M. Oakeshott, 1975, The vocabulary of a modern European state, Political Studies 23(2–3), 319–41.

they interact with other people and have responsibilities to them, as parents, brothers and sisters, classmates and so on. A society is not like a family or even a geographical community; it is a network of networks, a group of all the other groups. People are bound to society not by one big tie, like the legal status of a resident citizen, but many smaller ones.

The term 'pro-social behaviour' comes from social psychology. It is intended to refer to a wide range of actions in which people do things for the benefit of others rather than themselves, and in particular the circumstance in which people will try to help others directly. The area of interest for psychologists is not the same as for sociologists; it is to consider why some people help when others do not. The psychological literature has some interesting things to say about this. A classic study by Latané and Darley identified a series of conditions: the recognition that there was a situation in which help is required, the recognition of personal involvement and the cost of intervention.[11] None of this is really an argument for formal provision to be made – except, perhaps, as an insight into the limitations of relying on individual charity – and so it cannot be taken as an argument for or against the provision of welfare.

However, individual motivation is rather a poor test of the way that people behave. Many of the things that people do in society are not thought through, rationalised or clearly attributed to any motivation, altruistic or selfish. People are socialised. They learn to do things without thinking, or having to think, because they cannot walk around in a state of permanent moral crisis about every individual action and still hope to get dressed, washed or eat. "Prejudice", Burke wrote, "is of ready application in the emergency; it previously engages the mind in a steady course of wisdom and virtue, and does not leave the man hesitating in the moment of decision, sceptical, puzzled, and unresolved. Prejudice renders a man's virtue his habit; and not just a series of unconnected acts."[12] One of our many prejudices is to help other people in need, and it is no bad thing that we have it.

People might engage in pro-social behaviour from a sense of obligation or duty. Duties are complex, and the explanations people give about why they feel obligated are sometimes indirect. It is still not unusual in charities for their actions to be seen in terms of an obligation to the founders rather than to a client group. Some people accept responsibilities on behalf of others – standing in place of a parent or a spouse. Some will emphasise a legal duty

---

11. B. Latané and J. Darley, 1970, The unresponsive bystander, New York: Appleton-Century-Crofts.

12. E. Burke, 1790, Reflections on the revolution in France, New York: Holt, Rinehart and Winston, 1959, pp. 105–6.

as a trustee or a contractor. Some people will talk about their profession or their employment. Very few people will claim to do good because they are good people.

One of the key attempts to explain what kinds of obligations and ties these are has been framed in terms of reciprocity. When they receive things, people come under an obligation to make a return. The most obvious form of reciprocity is the direct exchange of goods – every commercial transaction is an exchange. However, it also extends to the exchange of gifts, and in societies in which cash is not the primary unit of exchange, it may involve other sorts of exchange – notably the exchange of members of the household. Less obvious, but no less widely practised, is 'generalised' reciprocity, in which people do not look for a direct return, but expect the return from somewhere else in the network. In a family, what goes around comes around; people contribute more or less freely, with the expectation that if they are ever in need, they will be able to rely on the others. Children owe duties to their parents, and that follows from direct exchange, but there are other chains of generalised reciprocity. Between generations, people look after their parents and they expect their children to look after them in turn. People look after their children, and they expect their children to look after their own children in turn. That means there are three directions of obligation: obligations now, obligations to those who have gone before and obligations to those who come after. The same things apply in the wider community, though they are not as strong as they are to those who are close to us – that is a big part of what being 'close' means.

Reciprocity is a major element in the glue that holds societies together; it has been seen as something that is almost universal, found in every society from tribes through to complex modern societies.[13] Arguably reciprocity defines society – the bonding of families, of communities and of nations is based on a complex set of networks of solidarity and mutual responsibility. One of the criticisms made of the literature on altruism is that in the vast majority of cases, it is possible to see humanitarian action in some sense as a mechanism of exchange – people get a sense of personal reward, achievement and status.

In *The Gift Relationship*, Richard Titmuss focused on the gift of blood, and part of the study is based on an argument that blood is more plentiful and better quality when it is donated than when it is bought and sold in a market. More importantly, Titmuss saw blood as a marker of a more general commitment to other people. Some of the reasons people gave Titmuss for giving blood may make sense as a form of exchange, after a fashion; people

---

13. A. Gouldner, 1960, The norm of reciprocity, American Sociological Review 25(2), 161–77.

might say they are doing it "to get a cup of tea" (which modestly downplays the gift) or that they see the donation as a sort of insurance: "I have a motor bike and someday I may need blood to help me." Other comments make little sense directly: "No money to spare. Plenty of blood to spare."[14] It is possible to see an element of reciprocity in this, but that may be reading too much meaning into the words – people are just finding something to say to explain something that feels right. Altruistic behaviour in everyday life is liable to fall outside the conventional terms of moral discourse; it is just what people do, and they don't have to rationalise it.

'SOMETHING MUST BE DONE'

It is common enough to hear arguments that needs ought to be met. The idea of 'need' brings together two discrete issues. Part of the idea of need is that people have a problem: dementia, unemployment, sickness or poverty are treated as categories of need. Part of the idea is that people ought to have a service; it makes perfectly good sense to talk about people's needs for counselling, hospital beds or an electricity supply. Properly speaking, need refers to the relationship between the two elements – a problem and a response to that problem. Needs are claims: saying that people are 'in need' implies that there should be some kind of action. When people say that there is a need, they are not just saying that there is an issue, but that something ought to be done about it.[15]

One of the most basic drivers of welfare provision is the sentiment that 'something must be done'. Welfare services do not provide for every need: when people are lonely, there is no obligation to offer them company, and when they are bereaved, nothing in the structure of services promises to provide them with alternative relationships. The problems that are being responded to are identified as social problems. In many cases, problems which are now commonly addressed by welfare states – poverty, old age, unemployment and child neglect – might in past times have been thought of as private or personal, and nothing to do with other people. There are likely to be some areas under dispute, and the answer may be different in different countries: the care of newly born children, smoking and obesity are examples of behaviours that were formerly thought of as private, and in some countries still are, but have been shifting into the public sphere. It has been possible, in different countries, to watch as definitions change. Domestic violence used to be thought of as a private matter, but it is coming to be thought of as a social

---

14. Titmuss, 1970.
15. P. Spicker, 1993a, Needs as claims, *Social Policy and Administration* 27(1), 7–17.

problem. Funerals are mainly treated as private affairs in Western countries, but there is an argument for a more socialised approach. On the other hand, the quality of housing or access to information used to be thought of as public issues, and in the United Kingdom at least they have been returning to the private sphere. That does not mean that there is no problem – only that it is not the sort of problem that demands a public response.

The suggestion that 'something should be done' begs the question of who should do it. The literature on helping behaviour makes a telling point: before people help, they will look to see who else is around and who else should take responsibility.[16] There is a strong tendency to look to public organisations to act, because that is why they are there, and after all they are the ones who have the competence and the responsibility. The specific responsibilities of government are considered in chapter 7. But the feeling that 'something must be done' is not a good way to manage public affairs. Does something have to be done if it cannot be done well or effectively – or even if it will do more harm than good? There are indeed some social services which are not done particularly well. The systems that exist to protect children from abuse by their parents are unreliable and there has been a long series of scandals in which misjudgements have been made. The provision of residential child care has had generally disappointing outcomes for children who grow up in it. If morality was only a matter of consequences, that would be a knock-down argument against intervention – but taking action is not just about what works. It also matters that we should try.

RIGHTS

The claims that people make for service are often framed not just in terms of need, but also of rights. When people have rights, it shapes the way that other people are supposed to behave towards them. Some of the principles behind rights were introduced in chapter 2. There are three main categories of rights:

• *Particular rights.* Particular rights, such as rights under a contract, apply only to specific people in specific circumstances. That may seem to have limited scope for welfare, but the opposite is true – this is a very common arrangement for pensions, and many countries organise medical care on similar principles.

---

16. Latané and Darley, 1970.

- *General rights.* General rights affect everyone under the law, usually the citizens of a country. Examples, where they apply, are minimum incomes, access to hospitals or schooling.
- *Human rights.* Human rights apply to everyone, wherever they are. Human rights have been developed through international agreements. They are enforced through national jurisdictions and are held to apply to people in all circumstances, regardless of nationality or personal status.

The case for welfare is partly that it is required to respect the rights that citizens hold, and partly that it is needed to respect the rights that everyone has.

There are important differences between the discourse of rights and the discussions of altruism and obligation which went before. The first is that rights are supposed to inhere in the people who benefit from them. Obligations or duties, such as the duty of charity, are determined by other people: if someone has a charitable duty to help me, it does not follow that I have any right to the help. Rights are held by the person who is most likely to be interested in them. While there are rights which impose duties on other people, others do not. Liberties protect and legitimise the activities of the rights-holder, and immunities (such as a disabled parking badge) allow freedom to some people that others do not have. Privileges give people options that other people may not have – a driving licence is a privilege.

The second feature of rights, which matters greatly in practice, is that rights are meant to be enforceable. There may be some rights which are nothing more than assertions – the right to work, the right to respect – but the three classes of rights mentioned here (particularly the rights of citizenship and human rights) have in common that they are subject to law and open to redress – that is, able to be challenged and to get things set straight when they go wrong. Redress is basic to the 'rule of law' – without it, there is no reason to assume that the law will be complied with. There comes a point when moral obligation is translated into concrete, legal duties, and the way that rights have developed has made this one of the most important ways in which the weakest and most vulnerable people can be protected.

At the same time, it is important to acknowledge that some of the rights considered here are defeasible – they can be annulled or cancelled if certain conditions are not satisfied. That is especially true of particular rights – people who break a contract in one way cannot rely on the same contract in another – but it is also commonly applied to rights of citizenship, in which people who have broken social rules (for example, by committing criminal offences or antisocial behaviour) may have other rights suspended. Many politicians accept Mead's argument that rights to welfare have to be counterbalanced by obligations,[17] and that position has been influential in a range of countries, where welfare reform, 'workfare' and 'activation' of the unemployed have been strongly associated with 'conditionality' or the imposition of moral tests.[18] Only universal rights, of which human rights are the main model, are not subject to reservations of this sort.

THE MAIN ARGUMENTS FOR WELFARE IN CHAPTER 3

It is good to do things for other people, whether this is done out of humanitarianism, charity, duty or a sense of social responsibility.

Sometimes we feel, morally, that something must be done, that people are in need and that state or social organisations have to take action.

People have a range of rights to welfare – particular rights gained from interaction, exchange and contract, rights of citizenship and human rights.

---

17. L. Mead, 1992, The new politics of poverty, New York: Basic Books.
18. P. Dwyer, 2004, Creeping conditionality in the UK, Canadian Journal of Sociology 29(4), 265–87; J. Clasen and D. Clegg, 2007, Levels and levers of conditionality, in J. Clasen and N. Siegel (eds.), Investigating welfare state change, Cheltenham: Edward Elgar.

Chapter Four

Individualism and Self-Interest

Individualism is often presented as reason to oppose the welfare state. Liberal political thought begins with the freedom of the individual. The thinkers of the New Right – the 'neo-liberals' – have argued that the liberty of individuals is safeguarded best by leaving people to their own devices and limiting the role and size of the state.[1] (American conservatives confusingly use the word 'liberal' in the opposite sense, to refer to people who want government to be more active.) Neo-liberals interpret the idea of freedom in a restrictive way: they assert that freedom consists entirely of freedom from interference, and claim that it extends to control over property and nothing else. The first part of that formulation is clearly inadequate. All freedom, Maccallum argues, is freedom of a person, from restraint, to do something.[2] The power to make choices and the power to act are basic. The power to make choices calls for people to be able to function as individuals – which is why children have to be educated, why people cannot sell themselves into slavery and why addiction is inimical to freedom. The power to act is about capacity: it matters what people can do and how. Taken together, these two elements are essential to autonomy, and autonomy is fundamental to individualism.[3]

The second part of the neo-liberal argument, the assertion of property rights, is curiously selective. Property rights clearly do matter; they are important for autonomy, capacity and personal security. The denial of property rights to women in parts of Africa is a major part of the disadvantage that

---

1. See, for example, F. Hayek, 1960, The constitution of liberty, London: Routledge and Kegan Paul.

2. G. Maccallum, 1967, Negative and positive freedom, Philosophical Review 76, 312–34.

3. See P. Spicker, 2006a, Liberty, equality, fraternity, Bristol: Policy Press.

women experience. One has to ask, though, why writers like Nozick and Hayek should elevate property rights to the highest status (Hayek recognises the conditional and social character of property rights[4]), while disregarding the importance of other rights – rights such as the much-criticised rights to a family life, income security or access to medical care, all enshrined in the Universal Declaration of Human Rights.

RATIONAL SELF-INTEREST

The economic literature has been dominated in recent years by a model of 'rational' individual choice. Rational individuals are able to make complex choices instantly, consistent in their judgements, perfectly informed and in-different to the effects on everyone else. Those claims are unrealistic, but the assumptions at least produce some usable predictions of behaviour. It is less defensible to accept that the rational individual wants more of everything[5] – hospital care, deep-fried food, perambulators, heat – when sane people often want less; that rational people have no objection to other people having many more resources than them,[6] when this could exclude them from the division of goods; or that everything has its price. Those claims are absurd, because they work in the opposite direction from self-interest or individual welfare.[7]

The study of rational self-interest assumes not just that people will choose things that benefit them at the expense of others, but that they will not want to accept responsibility for the needs of other people. Even if that were true – the argument is not consistent with the ideas discussed in the previous chapter – it would not follow that 'rational' individuals do not co-operate with others. A simple example might be taken from the private sector: the role of the factor or building manager. Where people have apartments in a building or own property that is part of an integrated development, it is not uncommon for them to be obliged, as a condition of ownership, to contribute to a mutual fund covering maintenance, common areas and possibly more. ('Factors' in Scotland are agents who commonly cover issues such as communal lighting, cleaning and buildings insurance.) The reason why this kind of arrangement is set up is partly down to convenience – it takes much more effort to arrange these things separately – but it is generally cheaper than trying to do things individually, and it is also a reflection of the way that the behaviour and prop-

---

4. F. Hayek, 1948, Individualism and economic order, Chicago: University of Chicago Press.
5. A. Anderton, 1997, Economics, Ormskirk: Causeway Press, p. 83.
6. For example, J. Griffin, 1986, Well-being, Oxford: Oxford University Press, p. 147.
7. P. Spicker, 2013, Reclaiming individualism, Bristol: Policy Press.

erty maintenance undertaken by each tenant affects the position of everyone else. There are privatised systems used in some countries for the distribution of drinking water, sanitation and the development of access roads. Almost inevitably the externalities, the duplication of effort, the inconvenience and the inconsistent supply of services means that these are inferior arrangements to collective ones. Collective arrangements make sense, and if the choices and processes which lead to them being set up are legitimate, so are the arrangements. Many of the services provided by governments fall into similar categories. Examples include the provision of roads, power, street lighting and cleaning, amenity spaces, waste disposal and common security.

A common objection to collective provision is a reference to the position of the 'free rider' – the individual who takes from the group without giving back. Self-interested individuals, the argument runs, won't stick with the rules: they will cheat because that way they will draw more out of the system than they put in.[8] The "tragedy of the commons", Hardin suggests, is that it is in the interests of individuals to overuse the amenities. Eventually, the structure will collapse.[9] Many of the 'games' designed by economists are designed to prove this point.[10]

There are four key objections to this argument. The first is based on self-interest. What people gain from public arrangements – roads, sewers and so on – is much greater than they can possibly hope to achieve through their own efforts.

The second objection is based on morality. Human beings do not behave much like the supposedly rational individuals of economic theory, who are driven by a sense of sociopathic irresponsibility. The norm of reciprocity is found throughout human societies. The most basic protection against people taking advantage of the commons is that people do not think it is right, and human society cannot be understood without that basic sense of right and wrong. Hardin misrepresents the nature of collective action. He writes, "Consider bank robbing. The man who takes money from a bank acts as if the bank were a commons."[11] This view of the 'commons' is nothing like common property: it is a lawless no-man's land. Hardin seems to think that grazing a cow on common land and robbing a bank are both done without reference to other people, and that is nonsensical. Robbing banks is done with the intention of depriving other people of things they have. Common property

---

8. M. Olson, 1971, The logic of collective action, Cambridge, MA: Harvard University Press.

9. G. Hardin, 1968, The tragedy of the commons, in R. Kuenne (ed.), Readings in social welfare, Oxford: Blackwell, 2000.

10. For example, A. Poteete, M. Janssen and E. Ostrom, 2010, Working together, Princeton, NJ: Princeton University Press, ch. 2.

11. Hardin, 1968, Oxford: Blackwell, 2000, p. 159.

is property that is shared with other people; it depends on rules, and it has to be managed collectively.

The third objection concerns the assumptions about free riders. There may be free riders in some spheres of activity, because it is sometimes possible for people to default; for example, in some professions there is often a 'brain drain' in which people trained at the expense of one country go off to seek rewards from another. But the brain drain runs mainly from poorer countries to richer ones, because what the migrants are able to do is to use their human capital to join a richer club. They are not defaulting by opting out of collective arrangements; they are opting in to other ones.

The fourth, and possibly the most important, objection is based on experience. Many groups based on mutual support and common ownership have lasted for generations. Hayek, one of the strongest supporters of the conservative individualism associated with the New Right, still condemned

> the silliest of the common misunderstandings: the belief that individualism postulates (or bases its arguments on the assumption of) the existence of isolated or self-contained individuals, instead of starting from men whose whole nature and character is determined by their existence in society.[12]

Real people are not automatons or calculating machines. People who live in society learn to use its rules, structures and techniques to achieve their ends. As such, they interact, they exchange and they cooperate.

MUTUALITY AND SOCIAL PROTECTION

The principle of mutuality is in large part a recognition of common self-interest; to the extent that everyone receives protection, everyone benefits. One of the basic instruments used to deliver collective support to individuals in this way is insurance. There are various reasons why people might see this as being in their individual interests, but for the most part the benefits are obvious: people pay insurance to reduce uncertainty about the future and to reduce their vulnerability to future events. That includes both events which are unforeseen, like being the victim of crime or disease, and others which are generally foreseeable, such as provision for old age. There are some forms of insurance that are highly individualised – where the contribution that each person is asked to make is calculated according to the individual level of risk that a person is subject to – but what makes it insurance is the sharing of risks

---

12. Hayek, 1948, p. 6.

with other people. It cannot be assumed that bad things, the sort of things that lead to people claiming benefits or receiving help from welfare services, only happen to other, less rational, people. By joining mutual arrangements, rational people make themselves less vulnerable to future harm.

Much has been made in contemporary literature of the new risks and insecurities associated with individualised societies, 'flexible' labour markets and precarious labour.[13] These problems are important, but they are by no means new: the systems developed during successive 'industrial revolutions' made extensive use of casual labour, often lacking the rights and protections that were introduced as a response. In many places, the systems of support were developed through mutual aid, either through trades unions or through mutual societies.[14] Social insurance is now commonly offered by governments, but government did not devise these systems. States, when they became involved in the process, had two options: either to build on the arrangements which had developed or to seek to replace them. In the United Kingdom, government opted to replace many of these mutualist arrangements – displacing, for example, the role of the Friendly Societies in the provision of health care. In France, the state battened its *régime général* on to existing networks of support, and left other issues, notably unemployment insurance, in the hands of 'social partners' (employers and trades unions) rather than government.

Mutualism does not have much of a problem with free riding: those who don't contribute don't get. The most basic weakness in this kind of system is the converse – that because it does not provide for free riders, it cannot offer comprehensive coverage or protection. It is exclusive as well as inclusive. It defines the contributors and the potential recipients as members of a club. The people who get left out – in the terms of French social policy, the 'excluded' – are often the poorest and most vulnerable. One of the key arguments for state intervention is that these systems need to be extended to include more people.

Many welfare systems take the form of social protection, possibly in the form of insurance, possibly expressed as entitlements of citizenship. In the European Union,

> Social protection systems . . . protect people against the risks of inadequate incomes associated with unemployment, illness and invalidity, parental responsibilities, old age or inadequate income following the loss of a spouse or parent. They also guarantee access to services that are essential for a life in dignity.[15]

---

13. For example, U. Beck, 1992, Risk society, London: Sage; and see M. Mullard and P. Spicker, 1998, Social policy in a changing society, London: Routledge.

14. P. Baldwin, 1990, The politics of social solidarity, Cambridge: Cambridge University Press.

15. European Observatory of Working Life, 2011, Social protection, http://www.eurofound .europa.eu/observatories/eurwork/industrial-relations-dictionary/social-protection.

The 'protective' element in social protection is sometimes identified with a 'safety net', provision in circumstances in which people are unable to make provision for themselves through their own or their family's resources. Poor laws, social assistance and discretionary assistance are generally considered forms of safety net provision, associated with what has become known as a 'residual' model of welfare. Even in fully developed systems of welfare, however, there is still a need for residual benefits and services – provision for those who are not covered in other ways.

Social protection includes safety nets, but it goes beyond them. Social insurance is used to maintain income, and arguably to redistribute it, in circumstances in which it is otherwise liable to be interrupted – unemployment, incapacity for work and old age. It is also used to provide funding for services so that contributors can claim funding or reimbursement at the time of need, for example to meet medical bills. And it can be used to provide services directly so that every insured person is able to draw on the provision made by the service. The mechanism is essentially redistributive: what people pay in is different from what they draw out. It might also be seen as redistribution between different periods in a person's life. Because so much that is done in systems of social protection is for pensioners, the systems have been interpreted as a form of 'income smoothing' – taking resources from one part of a person's life to protect them in other parts. And then there is the provision of security for people who would otherwise be vulnerable. This is sometimes couched in the language of 'risk', but the issue is not so much to avoid risk as to reduce vulnerability – the likelihood that when the risk becomes a reality, people will suffer as a result.

There is a widespread assumption in the critical literature that welfare provision is an imposition. The opposite is true: given choices as to how to safeguard their self-interest, rational individuals choose to engage in collective provision for social protection. That is how welfare provision typically develops. In his book *Charge!*, Arthur Seldon, another key figure in the movement to develop markets in place of state welfare, offered a challenge to his readers: "if you wouldn't leave your family without protection, what makes you think that other people would?"[16] Just so. That is how welfare systems developed in most of Europe: in the absence of collective provision, people made the arrangements they needed to make. However, people on very low incomes and insecure employment cannot necessarily afford to secure their position. Solidarity has developed gradually and progressively. The people who can afford to take part do so, but it is difficult to extend solidarity to the most vulnerable, and that is one of the key reasons

16. A. Seldon, 1977, Charge!, London: Temple Smith.

why compulsion has been introduced. It happened this way, for example, in France, where the various systems that provided for people in different occupations did not include most workers; that led to the development of the *régime général*, and when that was found in turn to leave others out, the development of systems for 'insertion' or inclusion. It is happening like this currently in the United States, where obligations to enrol in schemes for medical care have been introduced to extend the coverage of health insurance for people who are persistently excluded. Something similar happened in the Scandinavian countries, which developed social protection on a voluntary basis until the 1990s; compulsion was eventually introduced to balance the books.[17]

THE COMMON GOOD: INTERESTS IN COMMON

The idea that people share common interests is basic to many visions of society. It is expressed in many ways – the social harmony advocated by Robert Owen, the idea of a common weal, even in the kind of economics that judges human development through a series of indicators such as GDP. There are distinct elements of a common good. They include the interests which people have in common, the interests they share as members of a community or members of a society and the things which are needed for the maintenance and reproduction of a society.

The first of these is difficult to gainsay: individuals do have interests in common. Some of those common interests are human – human beings need to eat, to have shelter and so forth. Some are things that people learned to rely on, such as beds, telephones or refrigerators – the degree of consensus about 'essential' items is striking.[18] Others are communal, such as a general interest in a clean environment or shared use of communal facilities like roads, power supplies or cities. If the 'common good' is taken to mean that each person has an interest which others also have, it is based in the interests or welfare of each person individually. Social welfare has beneficial effects, not just for the people who receive services, but for others around them. Several examples spring to mind. National health systems offer support for people who are sick, which is a benefit to employers; in other countries, employ-

---

17. N. Ploug and J. Kvist (eds.), 1994, Recent trends in cash benefits in Europe, Copenhagen: Danish National Institute of Social Research.

18. See, for example, D. Gordon, L. Adelman, K. Ashworth, J. Bradshaw, R. Levitas, S. Middleton, C. Pantazis, D. Patisos, S. Payne Townsend and J. Williams, 1999, Poverty and social exclusion in Britain, York: Joseph Rowntree Foundation; P. Saunders, 2011, Down and out: poverty and exclusion in Australia, Bristol: Policy Press.

ers have to offer extensive health care facilities to protect their employees. Schooling prepares pupils for adulthood and develops their skills; the 'hidden curriculum' teaches obedience, habits of work and standards of behaviour.[19] Pensions make it possible for workers to retire, which is essential for the efficiency of the workforce.

The kinds of things that welfare states do in health, education or ensuring minimum standards in housing reflect this kind of common interest. It is just as true, however, to say that many interests are not shared or held in common, and there are liable to be problems as soon as differences between individuals are recognised. The dominant understandings of the 'common good' in economics are individualistic – for example, the 'greatest happiness of the greatest number', the idea of Pareto optimality used in welfare economics, or the maximisation of social value through cost/benefit analysis. All of those formulas start from the proposition that individual interests are in conflict and the interests of some are not going to benefit others. Where there are differences, any actions taken are for the good of some people, not everyone. Unless the rule is that every single person must benefit, the common good is not the good of everyone.

The second element, that people share interests as members of a society, is more contentious. There is such a thing as a collective entity. A family, a business, a school or an institution (such as the Catholic Church or the Norwegian Nobel Committee) are much more than groups of individuals; they are defined and understood, not just by the understandings and relationships of the people who are part of them, but by the way they act and behave, by their identity, the way that other people relate to them, their social existence. Wherever there are collective entities, it may be possible to speak about things being in their collective interests: things which make it possible to continue, things which allow them to prepare for the future, things which threaten their existence. There are, clearly, some collective entities which work in the interests of people who are engaged with them: that could be true of a school, a church, a voluntary organisation, a hospital or an employer. It is not difficult to see this kind of activity as an essential part of people's welfare, and one of the central understandings of 'poverty' concerns people's ability to participate in the society around them.[20]

The third element, the maintenance and reproduction of society, is not directly concerned with individuals at all; for that reason, it will be discussed later in chapter 9, which considers policies for society.

---

19. S. Bowles and H. Gintis, 1976, Schooling in capitalist America, London: Routledge and Kegan Paul.

20. P. Townsend, 1979, Poverty in the United Kingdom, Harmondsworth: Penguin, pp. 31–32.

RECLAIMING INDIVIDUALISM

What, then, does enlightened self-interest look like? No-one is really 'rational' in the economic sense, but self-interested individuals do not rely solely on their own resources. They pool their risks with others – for example, by buying insurance. Where they cannot do that, the sensible thing to do is to change the rules of the game so that they can. And that is what has happened throughout the developed world. Self-interest leads directly to welfare.

Individualism developed as a radical doctrine, standing in opposition to the established order. It is based, Locke argued, on the rights of the individual to life, liberty and property.[21] Some other terms might be the pursuit of happiness and personal dignity. In *Reclaiming Individualism*, I make an extended argument for measures which protect the circumstances of individuals: measures which are consistent with individualism, and may even be required by it. Table 4.1 is taken from that book.[22] Beyond the protection of rights, it argues for two other forms of action: the protection of basic security, because without security the capacity of individuals is undermined, and empowerment, so that people are able to exercise their rights effectively.

The table outlines four main positions that may lead individualists to support the provision of welfare. The universal standards – of which human rights, considered in chapters 2 and 3, are an example – are those things which are needed at the minimum for a person to function as an individual, for people to live with dignity, to make it possible for individuals to thrive

Table 4.1. Social Policy on Individualist Principles

	Rights	*Basic security*	*Empowerment*
Universal standards	Citizenship; human rights	Minimum income standards	Voting
Common interests	Community safety (e.g., fire services, coastguard)	Public health	Education
Shared objectives	Property rights; housing standards and provision	Securing economic prosperity; medical care	Access to information
Protecting individuals	Social care	Child protection; employment protection	Redress

21. J. Locke, 1690? Two treatises of civil government, P. Laslett (ed.), New York: Mentor, 1965.
22. Spicker, 2013.

and make choices. Common interests, in the second row of the table, are interests where the welfare of other people has a bearing on the welfare of individuals. Public health is an obvious example: the diseases of some people threaten the security of others. Shared objectives are aims that each individual will seek for themselves while others are pursuing the same objective. These objectives can be pursued in isolation, perhaps in competition, but they might also be done cooperatively; by collective provision, or pooling resources with others, they may well be better able to achieve their aims.

Those first three categories could all be defended in terms of self-interest, but, as the emphasis on universal standards suggests, individualism is bigger than that; it is also a defence of the position of each and every person. There is also a need to protect some individuals. The position of children is the clearest example. Their rights to life, liberty and happiness clearly depend on more than the absence of interference. There is not a state in the world that does not recognise duties to children, at least in the form of formal systems of education; education is fundamental to the development of the individual. Social work with families is a residual service, intended to offer protection to children who might in other circumstances have been able to look for support from a family member. 'Child protection' mainly refers to the situation of children at serious risk of abuse and neglect and those without the support of a family; it is sometimes extended to include dangers of involvement in crime. Many of the systems used for child protection are surprisingly recent in origin; many well-meaning professionals found it impossible and unnatural to believe that parents could willingly cause serious harm to their children, and child abuse had to be formally 'discovered' before intervention was considered permissible.[23]

There are many other examples, however. There are vulnerable people with failing faculties – for example, older people who suffer from dementia or people who are recovering from a stroke. Some adults suffer from mental illnesses, which reduce their capacity to make decisions. There are situations in which otherwise competent adults are vulnerable to abuse or exploitation – low-paid employment, debt, drug use and oppressive contracts. People's choices can be limited by their circumstances, and where that happens intervention can help to increase their autonomy.[24]

This is a different point from the idea of 'social protection' referred to in chapter 1. Social protection is generally understood in terms of a broad coverage of conditions and circumstances, such as the provision made for pensions

23. S. Pfohl, 2003, The 'discovery' of child abuse, in P. Conrad and V. Leiter (eds.), Health and health care as social problems, Lanham, MD: Rowman & Littlefield.

24. For an extended consideration of this argument, see Spicker, 2006a.

in old age. Systems of social protection reduce the range of vulnerability, but many of those systems also leave people out. One of the fundamental principles of individuals is that individuals matter – and that extends to each and every individual. No-one should be left behind. So the protective principle may come into effect when other systems stop. Any system which claims to value the individual needs a safety net – some provision for emergencies and exceptional circumstances – because without that, individuals will suffer.

THE MAIN ARGUMENTS FOR WELFARE IN CHAPTER 4

Welfare serves people's interests, and people who are self-interested tend to choose to have welfare.

People make collective arrangements with others for their mutual benefit and to further their common and shared interests. If the choices which lead to them being set up are legitimate, so are the arrangements.

Welfare furthers the common good – the interests which people have in common and the interests they share as members of a community or members of a society.

Some universal standards are needed for people to function as individuals, to live with dignity, and to make it possible for individuals to thrive and make choices.

There is also a need to protect some people.

Chapter Five

The Limits of the Market

The challenge to the welfare state has been strongest in those countries identified as 'liberal' welfare regimes, including the United States, Canada, Australia, the United Kingdom and New Zealand. Ruggie first described a liberal welfare state as one in which "the proper sphere of state behavior is circumscribed by the functioning of market forces."[1] Esping-Andersen extended the term to emphasise both an emphasis on market-based solutions and a limited acceptance of welfare provision. "Means-tested assistance, modest universal transfers, or modest social-insurance plans predominate . . . entitlement rules are strict and often associated with stigma; benefits are typically modest . . . the state encourages the market."[2]

In the last fifty years or so, the 'New Right', combining the laissez-faire economic policies of nineteenth-century liberals with some of the concerns of traditional conservatism, have put forward a strong message of support for markets and opposition to any activity that might 'distort' them.[3] Most of the arguments they make against 'welfare' are not about welfare as such; they are not objecting to the fact that people choose to spend money on issues like health, education or housing, if that is what they want to do. Their objections are made to the provision of such services on a collective basis rather than on market principles. Neo-liberals have seen public welfare as both a burden and a diversion of resources from the more legitimate preferences that would have been expressed in the market. They have argued for cutting back public expenditure and a shift in the balance of economic activity towards private enterprise.

1. M. Ruggie, cited in J. Quadagno, 1987, Theories of the welfare state, Annual Review of Sociology 13, 109 – 28.
2. G. Esping-Andersen, 1990, The three worlds of welfare capitalism, Cambridge: Polity, p. 26.
3. See, for example, N. Barry, 1987, The new right, Beckenham: Croom Helm; D. King, 1987, The new right, Basingstoke: Macmillan.

These arguments have influenced social policy very widely.[4] The McClure review in Australia emphasises alternatives to welfare – individual and family responsibility, support from employers and philanthropy from independent institutions.[5] Both Canada[6] and the United Kingdom[7] have gradually shifted, through years of retrenchment and modification of programmes, from a universalist base and stress on citizenship towards residualised systems. The fundamental proposition behind these positions is that, wherever it is possible to do so, social policies are best left to the market. That proposition is the subject of this chapter.

MARKETS AND WELFARE

'Markets' are based on the free operation and interaction of commercial provision and consumer demand. The main objection to the provision of collective public services rests in the belief that markets do things better. Economists have developed two 'fundamental theorems' of welfare. The first theorem claims to show that, under the conditions that apply in a market with perfect competition, people's welfare will be maximised. "The First Fundamental Theorem of Welfare Economics", Starr claims, "is a mathematical statement of Adam Smith's notion of the invisible hand leading to an efficient allocation."[8] The second theorem claims to show that markets can always deliver. "No matter which Pareto efficient state we specify", Sen explains, "it is possible to have a competitive market equilibrium yielding precisely that state, by choosing the initial distribution of resources appropriately."[9] Starr draws from that the conclusion that "public authority intervention in the market through direct provision of services (housing, education, medical care, child care etc.) is an unnecessary escape from market allocation mechanisms with their efficiency properties."[10] Taken together, the 'Fundamental Theorems of Welfare' claim to show that markets can always be organised so as to deliver just what

---

4. See, for example, H. Glennerster and J. Midgley (eds.), 1991, The radical right and the welfare state, Brighton: Harvester Wheatsheaf; J. Myles, 1998, How to design a 'liberal' welfare state: a comparison of Canada and the United States, Social Policy and Administration 32(4), 341 – 64.

5. Reference Group on Welfare Reform to the Minister for Social Services, 2015, A new system for better employment and social outcomes, Canberra: Department for Social Services.

6. K. Battle, 1998, Transformation: Canadian social policy since 1985, Social Policy and Administration 32(4), 321 – 40.

7. P. Taylor Gooby and T. Larsen, 2004, The UK – a test case for the liberal welfare state? in P. Taylor Gooby (ed.), New risks, new welfare, Oxford: Oxford University Press.

8. R. Starr, 1997, General equilibrium theory, Cambridge: Cambridge University Press, p. 146.

9. A. Sen, 1993, Markets and freedoms, Oxford Economic Papers 45(4), 519 – 41, p. 521.

10. Starr, 1997, p. 151.

people want. If, in principle, things can be done just as well without the development of formal public institutions, then it seems to follow that either needs will be met through the market or, if people do not have the resources, that the situation can be corrected by a redistribution of money. In either case, there is no real need for collective organisation to provide services.

The key weaknesses of this argument lie in some rather arcane definitions of 'welfare' and 'efficiency'. 'Welfare' in economic theory is not a test of whether or not people have basic well-being, such as food to eat: it is a question of whether or not the allocation they get is compatible with the preferences they express, regardless of whether they have any resources to get what they want. People can be starving, homeless or refugees, and it is not relevant to their welfare within this theory. 'Efficiency' is usually interpreted in terms of a settled distribution of goods: an allocation is 'Pareto optimal' if no-one can be made better off without making someone else worse off. Ryan comments:

> there are innumerable Pareto-efficient situations which strike observers as intolerable. . . . An economy in which all resources belong to one person and everyone else is starving to death is Pareto efficient, since there is no way in which anyone's welfare can increase without someone else's diminishing. It is also repulsive.[11]

Even within the narrow confines of this theory, markets cannot and do not deliver an ideal distribution. The main deficiency of market provision which is identified in economics textbooks goes under the name of 'market failure' and refers to conditions in which markets cannot do what the theory supposes they will be able to do. Unless there is perfect information and no locational costs, and unless goods and services can be treated as saleable commodities, the market may not deliver as planned. One problem lies in 'externalities', in which people gain or lose by a process which is not being considered part of the market decision. It may be possible to make more money, for example, by polluting the environment; much effort has been devoted to attempts to refine market processes to make sure that polluters pay. The benefits of education are felt throughout the wider society; that is one reason why just about every country has arranged for education to be provided publicly, rather than leaving it to the decision of individual families. Another example lies in 'public goods', like parks and street lighting. If they are not divisible and not exclusive, there is no practical way of matching the use of the facility to a proportionate payment.

The guidance from the UK Treasury about government intervention presupposes that market failure is the primary reason for intervention.

---

11. A. Ryan, 1989, Value judgements and welfare, in D. Helm (ed.), The economic borders of the state, Oxford: Oxford University Press, p. 47.

Before any possible action by government is contemplated, it is important
to identify a clear need which it is in the national interest for government to
address. Accordingly, a statement of the rationale for intervention should be
developed. This underlying rationale is usually founded either in market failure
or where there are clear government distributional objectives that need to be
met. Market failure refers to where the market has not and cannot of itself be
expected to deliver an efficient outcome; the intervention that is contemplated
will seek to redress this. Distributional objectives are self-explanatory and are
based on equity considerations.[12]

Where there are distributional issues, the answer is not intervention but to
take steps to alter the distribution, usually by offering people extra income.
That is how to deal with shortages of food, clothing or fuel. If market failure
is the primary reason accepted for intervention, it rests on an assumption that
markets will normally provide, and do it well enough.

The concept of 'market failure', however, largely misses the point. Markets
cannot do everything – it is in their nature that they should not. Much of the
literature attaches a considerable weight to 'choice', and the central insight
that readers are supposed to take away with them is the idea that markets
offer choice to consumers. This passes over the other central element of the
economic theory used to support the idea of the market: that producers have
choices too. They can decide what they are going to produce and how much of
it. Part of what happens in any market is that producers make decisions about
where they will work, who they will work for and what they are ready to do
at the price offered. That means – it must mean – that producers leave gaps.
Consumers only get to choose the things that producers are prepared to offer.
Currently, for example, the world seems ready to be running short of treatments for snakebites, which kill about 100,000 people in Africa every year: the
firm that used to produce the antidote has opted to focus on rabies treatments
instead, and it will take other firms several years to develop the facilities to
enter the market.[13] There is no reason here to criticise the supplier; they are doing what commercial firms are expected to do. If markets fail to reach people,
it is not necessarily a sign that they are not working; it might well be because
they are doing what they are supposed to do.

Wherever producers have a choice, some people will not get a service:
that is built into the model. Who those people are depends on the potential
returns, but often the people who are not served are those who have special-
ised needs, who present special problems, who live in difficult locations or

---

12. HM Treasury, n.d., Green Book, London: HM Treasury.
13. BBC, 2015, Snakebite antidote is running out, http://www.bbc.co.uk/news/health-34176581.

are otherwise difficult to deal with. There may be a desire to avoid 'moral hazard', where people effectively demand more service as a result of their own choices and actions. There is a process of exclusion, sometimes referred to as 'adverse selection'. So if we want, as a matter of policy, to ensure that such circumstances are treated regardless of the choices made by producers, it makes sense to look to collective, non-market arrangements. Psychiatric care is an example; it is not particularly expensive in the short term, but the costs mount up, reflecting long periods of treatment and uncertain outcomes. In the United States, often seen (questionably) as the very model of a private health care system, psychiatric care is commonly provided for by state governments, because there is no practical way of getting it covered by the market.

It does not follow that markets have to be superseded altogether. There are many circumstances when the theory works – for example, in the production and distribution of food. There are few people who would argue for a National Food Service. If people cannot get food, they will usually be offered extra income to buy it. The idea of social security – providing people with cash rather than services – assumes implicitly that there is a functioning market. Markets can do a lot. If a government department needs paperclips, it does not go into the business of producing paperclips: it buys them commercially, like any other organization would. In the same way, the argument runs, the private sector can be commissioned to provide houses, schools or medical treatment.

This is for the most part a practical matter, and the relative costs are often decisive. In health, social care, education and transport – areas where privatisation is reintroducing commercial operators or developed markets for the first time – the arguments for private provision are usually selective. In the development of social policy, markets are rarely supplanted altogether: they may need to be supplemented, and they may need substantially to be replaced. That leads not to a state in which government does everything, but to welfare pluralism – a 'mixed economy' of welfare.

SERVICES

There is another important gap between theory and practice: the role of personal service. The 'personal social services', including social care and child protection, have sometimes been treated as peripheral to the work of the welfare state, but they have played an increasingly large role over the course of the last fifty years. Some elements of these services can be met by production and transfer of goods, but that is not what happens in the main. Services depend on a process of continuing contact and support. Economic production happens when a good is made; goods like food or clothing can sit on shelves until they are bought. This is not how services work. The key element in a service, Osborne and his colleagues argue, is that production and consumption happen at the same time – and so that it is not possible to offer someone a service without that person being present or at least engaged in the process.[14]

Confining the discussion for the moment to the private sector – or more precisely to commercial provision for profit – there are some obvious problems in trying to adapt an idealised model of production to the interpretation of service provision. In the first place, the choices open to private service providers are limited. A producer can make more or less of a good, hold it in stock or run stocks down, choose the time when it comes to market. A service provider, by contrast, will find it very difficult to manage the quantity of service provided, and although there are services which hold the capacity for provision in reserve, it is difficult to do. The choices that are open to service providers are much more about limiting demand. They can limit the amount of time they give people. They can make people wait to ensure that there is a flow of demand. They can make decisions about who best fits the character of service they offer and divert prospective customers to other services. Those are, of course, commonly used ploys in the provision of public services as well.

A second, widely occurring issue is that many services are highly regulated. People cannot, in most developed countries, simply set themselves up as a dentist or a surgeon and offer their services. Milton Friedman once argued that doctors should be managed through the free market, without regulation: regulation restricted the supply of doctors, and anyway people might occasionally benefit by going to quacks.[15] Friedman deliberately chose an extreme example to make the point, but the problem is not about the role of government, but rather the kinds of restrictions that limit the scope of 'free markets' in practice.

The third problem follows from the importance of direct personal contact. Effective services depend on access to the person served; they depend on establishing a relationship. There are some services which allow consumers to hop between service providers – insurance, hotels, catering and taxis are examples. There are private sector services in which this kind of relationship has not been problematic: people stay with the same bank for years, they are often locked into long-term contracts for phones or domestic services. For other services, however, and particularly for those services associated with the provision of welfare, this principle is not easily extended. Relatively simple services like cleaning or hairdressing might be done on an ad hoc basis, but even there, as a general proposition, lack of continuity detracts from

---

14. S. Osborne, Z. Radnor and G. Nasi, 2013, A new theory for public service management? American Review of Public Administration 43(2), 135 – 58.

15. M. Friedman, 1962, Capitalism and freedom, Chicago: University of Chicago Press, chap. 9.

the quality of service. This has become a major problem for the provision of domiciliary services to older people. Treating domiciliary care as a series of fifteen-minute packages of time helps firms behave as if they were letting out hotel rooms, but the approach also means that people can be faced with a bewildering series of care workers coming through their doors. Services cannot be fragmented without changing the character of the service provided. Support for older people in sheltered housing was originally intended to offer a degree of protection in the event of an emergency, such as a fall. As this service developed, it became evident that support staff were doing things that went beyond the job description – offering personal support, organising social activities, helping to negotiate with services – and that these, rather than the original purpose, were the sort of thing that was most valued by the service users.

One of the criticisms commonly made of the provision of welfare has been that there are problems of service quality, choice and control for service users. Indeed there are, but many of those issues are intrinsic to the kinds of things that welfare services are trying to do. The situation is more difficult to manage, because they often deal with people who are vulnerable, who lack a say in provision or who depend heavily on the personal elements of contact (such as the 'social bath', where a domiciliary care assistant or nurse helps someone to wash). The theoretical preference that many people express for market provision ultimately carries little weight. The demand for services cannot be met effectively as if they were commodities, and it is questionable whether markets can be adapted to overcome the problems. Having said that, the issues outlined here would present problems regardless of who provides services.

COMPETITION

Markets work in principle because there is competition. Consumers have a choice, and if an alternative product is cheaper or offers higher quality for the same price, they will choose that instead. Businesses have choices, and they will decide what to provide and how much according to what they can sell and how that compares to their competitors. Competition then leads to lower prices, higher quality and better choices.

It is not difficult to make hay with the assumptions behind the idea of 'perfect competition'. It is just not true that there is always competition, that businesses can enter and exit markets freely and that there are no local monopolies or transport costs to consider. Businesses are not rational economic actors any more than human beings are. For everyone who calculates a price in a way that will enhance profits, there is someone who thinks in terms of fair pricing, someone who compares the prices offered by competitors, someone who takes what they can get given their sunk costs and someone who bides their time. Competition is supposed to hold down costs, but in some cases it might increase them. It requires duplication of services, spare capacity, marketing, separate systems of finance and – of course – a margin for profit. Looking at the costs of public and private systems in health care, it tends to be true that substantially public services are likely to be cheaper and more tightly controlled than market-oriented systems (the French term is *la médicine libérale*). Indeed, one of the most telling criticisms of the UK National Health Service by the Institute of Economic Affairs is that its practices lead to under-funding in areas in which market provision would permit people to pay more for a service they prefer to have.[16]

Choice-based services rely on there being several options from which a choice can be made. In theory, what should happen is that the service user is offered a range of outcomes. When the Wagner report argued that residential care should be a "positive choice", it assumed not just that people would have a say, but that they would have preferences for group or individual living and the option to choose either.[17] This is not how things usually work. The choice for residential care is often made under constraint – in nearly half the cases, after hospital admission, decisions are commonly made by carers or professionals, not by service users; the critical decisions depend heavily on where there are vacancies. People who fund their own care generally have to settle for traditional services "either because better alternatives do not exist, or because people lack the information and advice to find them."[18] Shortages of provision, competition for resources and limited options make it difficult for choices to be exercised effectively, and people have to accept second-, third- or fourth-best options.

There are similar reservations to make about the claims that competition increases quality. Faced with rising costs and diminishing returns, private providers have strong incentives to avoid giving service, typically through exclusion and adverse selection. There are loads of examples in which private contractors skimp on service quality, because they are looking for shortcuts.[19]

---

16. K. Niemietz, 2015, What are we afraid of? Universal healthcare in market-oriented health systems, London: Institute for Economic Affairs.

17. G. Wagner, 1988, Residential care: a positive choice, London: HMSO.

18. ACEVO, cited in C. Needham, 2011, Personalising public services, Bristol: Policy Press, p. 95.

19. For example, Law Report: In the matter of capita translation and interpreting limited [2015] EWFC 5; F. Lawrence, 2013, Private health contractor's staff told to cut 999 calls to meet targets, The Guardian, 23 January; R. Whittell and M. Dugan, 2014, Services provider established by outsourcing giant Serco overcharged NHS by millions, Independent, 27 August; House of Commons Work and Pensions Committee, 2013, Can the work programme work for all user groups? House of Commons.

The problem is an obvious one: wherever the provision of service is speci-fied in a contract, the private contractor makes most profit by holding down costs. That is commonly done by reducing labour, reducing inputs or dilution – and, where they get those choices wrong, exiting from the market. To avoid those circumstances, what happens in many welfare states is that government, implicitly or explicitly, accepts higher costs on activities when they are un-dertaken at their behest and underwrites public services activities when they are commissioned from the private sector.

INDEPENDENT PROVISION

Businesses don't consistently behave in the way that many economics text-books seem to imagine. There are many different types of businesses, ranging from single operators through to complex organisations. Some businesses are set up as 'social enterprises', and they may be governed by policy in the same way as public sector organisations. Some businesses think that they are public services: that they are there to serve the community, that it isn't important that they make a profit on everything. Many larger businesses are engaged in

- the provision of occupational welfare, the provision of services to employ-ees and ex-employees. Examples include health provision for employees and occupational pensions;
- policy-making and processes of government, for example by participating in strategic partnerships or corporatist arrangements for welfare provision; and
- corporate social responsibility, in which private firms act to improve welfare in the wider society. This includes both philanthropic activity and promotion of communities.

Some of the patterns that businesses follow are not dissimilar, then, to the issues that affect the provision of welfare in general terms.

The role of independent providers stretches beyond a narrow understanding of 'business'. In the definition of public services, some voluntary organisa-tions work to a defined range of social objectives and have as much claim to be public services as governments do. Some voluntary organisations are non-profit enterprises (in European parlance, ASBLs or *associations sans but lu-cratif*) – the practical distinction between non-profits and businesses is limited. Some are mutuals, who operate by distributing services to paying members – for example, the building societies. There are still places in which 'voluntary' health provision refers to private or commercial provision of services.

In some respects, voluntary non-profit providers behave like businesses: they make choices about the range and scope of their activities, and they compete for resources on the basis of economy and quality. In other respects, they behave like public services: they have an established set of policies which determine the pattern of responses in a range of situations. Many of the practices of public services were developed long before the days of the welfare state through the actions of voluntary providers.

No welfare system functions without some independent providers, and most welfare systems will have a mix of services of different types – commercial, corporate and voluntary among them. All the arguments up to this point imply, however, that independent provision cannot be enough. The circumstances that welfare services have to deal with go beyond the range that might hope to be met by the interaction of rational consumers and producers: long-term services, difficult problems and delivery to vulnerable people among them. If people want to protect themselves from risks, if they have rights which mean that their needs should be met, if others want to offer protection or feel a moral responsibility to act – in any of these cases, reliance on independent provision alone cannot be enough. There must be at least some residual provision to deal with circumstances that are not otherwise dealt with. Often, because the service is expected to be comprehensive, residual patching is not enough. Something else has to be done.

THE MAIN ARGUMENTS FOR WELFARE IN CHAPTER 5

Markets sometimes 'fail', in the sense that they cannot work adequately.

The advantages claimed for markets cannot consistently be realised, because many of the situations that welfare provision has to deal with are different from the conventional representation of production and economic exchange. The demand for services cannot be met consistently and effectively through commodification and exchange.

There would be gaps even if markets were to function perfectly. Markets cannot do everything. Some other arrangement has to be made.

Chapter Six

Providing Public Services

Public services provide services to the public, obviously enough, but that is something that private providers also do. There is a difference between a local authority 'home help' who cleans houses for vulnerable older people and a cleaning firm that hires out cleaners; between a municipal scheme for refuse collection and commercial collection of rubbish for a fee; between a public library and a system for renting books or streaming videos. Being 'public' might seem to mean that the services are owned and controlled by government, but things are not so simple. The 'public sector' consists of organizations that are authorised and controlled by government, but not everything in the public sector is a public service: some publicly owned industries are businesses. Many public services are not run by government at all. Lots of charities and voluntary organisations—sometimes called the 'third sector'— provide public services too. What makes services public is not defined by the types of goods or services they provide, but by why and how they do it.

Public services are services developed for a public purpose. Wherever there is a public service, somebody has identified how the public ought to be served, and the services have been established and commissioned to do what they do. So, for example, a police service may be required to serve everyone in an identified locality; a postal service may be required to deliver to every address in the country; a social work service may be required to identify groups in need and, within a fixed budget, offer services in accordance with specified priorities. If people have rights, if everyone in the population is to be served or if people who otherwise would be left out are to be served, public services have to provide for them regardless. Businesses, in economic theory, choose their scope of operations, the type and character of work that they do and when and where to do it. Public services do not have the same choices. They have their objectives and scope specified for them. That is why they are there.

It is in the nature of public services that the people who pay for the services (such as government, charitable donors or members) are not necessarily the people who receive them. That means, because it is another way of saying the same thing, that public services are generally redistributive. (That does not mean that richer people pay for poorer people—there are examples of the opposite, and for example subsidies to higher education or rail transport can be 'regressive'.) Some public services are organised on a charitable basis; some are mutuals, in which risks are pooled; some are paid through taxation. The key difference between public and commercial services is that commercial services are based on direct exchange—people get what they pay for. Public services work to a different principle: they are there to benefit people, sometimes the general public, sometimes a specific group (such as older people, children, people with disabilities).

Because public services are set up to benefit people, they are operated as a trust. Businesses work in principle by establishing a link between the producer, who sells a service, and the customer, who buys it. In a trust, by contrast, the characteristic relationship is that A commissions B to benefit C. Typically the lines of accountability depend on the relationship between A (the commissioner) and B (the provider), rather than the relationship of either to C (the recipient). Some public services refer to their users as 'customers', but the term is inappropriate. The relationship between a merchant and a customer is voluntary and contingent—that is, they can be rejected or broken. In the public services, neither of those conditions necessarily applies. Many of the systems that exist in contemporary welfare states are based on attempts to empower recipients by offering rights and redress—that is, the power to challenge decisions and get them changed—in circumstances in which someone in the private market might otherwise choose to go elsewhere.

This all implies patterns of governance, accountability and relationships with service users that are very different from any conventional model of the provision of goods in the market. Boyne summarises the differences in terms of the organisational environment, goals, organisational structures and the values that apply—the 'public sector ethos'.[1] The aims of public services are decided by governments, voluntary committees or the foundation documents of charities—not, in most cases, by the agencies themselves. The principles they work by will usually be guided by some sense of public benefit and accepted canons about the way they should work, such as rights, procedural

---

1. G. Boyne, 2002, Public and private management: what's the difference? Journal of Management Studies 39(1), pp. 97–122.

fairness and integrity. The system of governance means that decisions about public policy are constrained by authority and accountable in those terms.

THE PUBLIC SERVICES:
GOVERNANCE, ACCOUNTABILITY AND FINANCE

There are often several different lines of accountability in public organisations—including legal, financial, professional and administrative structures—but for present purposes, it is 'democratic' or 'constitutional' accountability that matters most. The governance of public services is generally constitutional, in the sense that the lines of authorisation will be traceable to a source—a sovereign government, the establishment of a charity, the terms of a bequest. Every action on behalf of a public agency depends on a line of authority linking the activity back to a legitimate source—possibly a constitution, possibly a system of legislative authority, sometimes an electoral or participative process. The public services are built around a similar structure of accountability—the system of authorisation, recording and reporting—to be legitimate and compliant with the rules of public governance. There are some businesses with this kind of structure, in which a board and CEO require compliance in every specification and authority for all major variations, but it is not generally the case. It may well be possible, within the structure of a private firm, for someone to change behaviours, policies or approaches in order to achieve given ends. Those options are not generally open to managers in the public services. Those services which are in the public sector—that is, owned and controlled by government—are particularly liable to be restricted.

Financial operations, similarly, are liable to be restricted. The private sector is able to balance its books in other ways than the control of expenditure. There is usually the option of supplementing income through diversifying activities, taking loans, adjusting payments to owners and where necessary terminating loss-making activity. The options in the public services are much more limited and any of these possibilities may be barred. The language of 'income generation' tends in public services to be used in different ways from the private sector, such as soliciting donations, obtaining grants or increased funding allocations. Income generation in the sense of 'making money' is not, in general, an option. A service that makes excess income or builds up reserves is assumed to be failing to meet its primary objectives (which further supposes that making income is not one of those objectives). People who are strongly in favour of the profit motive and personal incentives in the private sector are likely to be concerned that allowing public services to make money will put the private sector at a disadvantage, and distort the operation of the market in related services.

WHY PUBLIC SERVICES ARE NOT LIKE BUSINESSES

The assumption is often made in public policy that business does things better, and that if public services were only run more like commercial enterprises, it would be better for all of us. A series of policies has been developed aiming to break up public services, to shift responsibility from the public services to private enterprise, to get public services to operate more like private ones or to try to replicate the conditions that have made businesses work in other spheres.

Public services are not like businesses, nevertheless. The aims of businesses are themselves extremely diverse, which makes it difficult to generalise, but it is widely accepted that businesses operate by making choices about what they do and how they do it. Businesses (and other firms working in the business environment, such as social enterprises) have to define their scope, the level of activity they are committed to and their operational processes according to the circumstances in which they will have to operate. The same is not true of public services. Public services do not choose their own objectives—the objectives are set for them. They cannot choose to do something just because they think it appropriate (a major block on innovation). Just as important, they cannot freely choose *not* to do things—a process which is critical to company behaviour and profit maximisation.

The effect of these conditions is to leave behind the usual models of economic behaviour. Despite the fashion for management by objectives, public services are not permitted to define their activity solely in terms of outcomes—that would not be compatible with constitutional government. They are not permitted to divert resources to alternative activities. The interests of providers are not in general met by generating a surplus of income over expenditure. The interests of consumers are not met by responding to market signals, because the purchasers are not the consumers. In the public sector, in particular, they cannot act without express authority.

The central test of whether public services are performing adequately is the test of *effectiveness*—whether they have met the aims which have been set for them. In a competitive market, private firms have to adapt what they do to the conditions of the market. They have to decide what to produce and how much, and if they cannot do it profitably, they have leave it to someone else. In the terms of standard economic theory, this means that businesses are constantly under pressure to be *efficient*—to produce units of production, or intended outcomes, at the lowest possible unit cost. If they do not produce enough, their costs will be higher than they should be; they will be unable to compete and could be driven out of the market. If they exceed their capacity for efficient production, unit costs start to rise and profits fall. That is why competition drives business to be more efficient.

In a public service, the same decisions are not eligible. The objectives are set and cannot be varied. The point is to achieve the aims of policy, not to op-timise the ratio of cost to output. That does not mean that they are profligate; most public services attempt to be *cost-effective*, achieving the aims of the service at the lowest cost. In nearly every case, however, cost-effectiveness and efficiency are different. The difference is most easily shown graphically. Figure 6.1, taken from my book *Policy Analysis for Practice*,[2] shows a model production function. Efficiency is maximised at the bottom of the curve. The most cost-effective approach, by contrast, depends on what the service is supposed to achieve. If it is supposed to cover the whole population, the

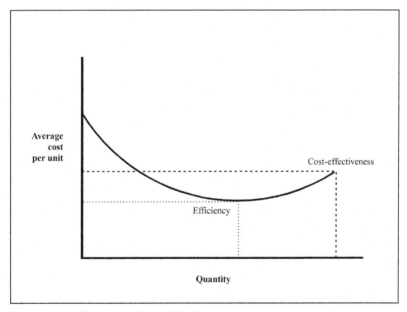

Figure 6.1. Efficiency and cost-effectiveness.

2. P. Spicker, 2006b, Policy analysis for practice, Bristol: Policy Press.

quantities provided will be fixed, even if it consequently costs more to reach everyone. Cost-effectiveness is typically found somewhere towards the right-hand edge of the curve, where average costs are higher, but aims are achieved to the maximum degree.

It is easy enough to see what this means in practice. Take, for example, a postal service. If the aim of the service is to make a profit, that can be done by selecting the routes in which there is most demand or the best return and avoiding others. Or consider social care services for older people: the obvious way to maximise profit is either to select the area of operation in which returns are optimised, typically avoiding people who are isolated, difficult to reach, uncooperative, who have the kinds of needs that drain services, or to provide services only if differential charges are levied. These options are not open to a public service operator.

Public services are often accused of being less efficient than private services. That is probably right. Public services are not trying to be efficient; they are trying to do something else. There is a trade-off to be made between efficiency and cost-effectiveness. When that happens, public services are supposed to choose the best way to meet their objectives, not to compromise them.

WHY WE NEED PUBLIC SERVICES

At this stage, it should be possible to answer one of the key questions about the provision of public services: Why should this kind of arrangement be made at all? Public services are there to carry out public policies, but there is some circularity in that proposition—that they are there because people have said they ought to be. It matters what public services are meant to do and who they are meant to do it for. One of the primary reasons why the services are necessary was explained in the previous chapter: if commercial markets are not able or willing to provide the things that ought to be done, someone else has to. If the process of provision is left to people who can choose whether or not to provide a service, some people will be left out altogether, while others will be served only on terms that may prove to be prohibitive. Some things may never happen at all, especially if they depend on payments from people who are poor, disadvantaged or excluded. Public services have often developed because governments or charities have wanted to fill the gaps. They cover the people who are not covered in a commercial market. In some cases, that is done on a residual basis: most people are left to their own devices, and public services pick out those who are left. That is the approach used for social care, child protection and employability support. In other cases, services are universal – they go to everyone, because that is a practical way of making sure that no-one is left out. Examples might be policing, fire fighting and coastguards. But universal provision is also done in cases in which residual provision might have been an option – education, because leaving out some children perpetuates disadvantage and limits freedom and opportunity, and health care, because residualised systems (like Medicaid in the United States, the support for people on low incomes) require a complex bureaucracy to operate.

There are at least four central circumstances in which public services are typically provided.

- Social goods, in which there is no practical way of charging individuals for the service but the benefits are felt collectively. Examples include policing, street lighting and flood protection.
- Circumstances in which there are minimum standards, implying that exceptions are not to be tolerated. This has included aspects of public health provision, the regulation of slum housing or compulsion related to water supply.
- Circumstances in which there is no realistic hope of basing a service on charges to users with limited resources, and third parties – typically governments or charities – have to pay: examples have been long-stay psychiatric care, the rehabilitation of offenders and long-stay care for older people.
- Circumstances in which the intention is to provide a service comprehensively to all – for example, public health provision, the collection of refuse and primary education.

Beyond that, there is a fifth justification for public services, which may be less compelling but is arguably more widely applicable: public service may simply be the best and most practical option for service delivery. In most developed countries, education services, social security and hospitals had their origins not in commercial or government activity but in voluntary, charitable and religious work: those beginnings have shaped the organisation, ethos and practice of public services for centuries. Any pragmatic or incremental development builds on the basis of what is there, and much of the work of the welfare states has been built on those foundations.

THE MAIN ARGUMENTS FOR WELFARE IN CHAPTER 6

Public services have developed to deliver services in ways that are compatible with public policy. Beginning with policy requires services to be directed to meet aims effectively and accountable in those terms.

Public services have been established and commissioned to do what they do. That means that they do not operate like theoretical businesses. They are redistributive and have to operate as a trust.

Public services may be developed

- to deliver social goods in circumstances in which markets do not operate,

- to ensure minimum standards,

- to develop services which users could not realistically pay for in their own right and

- to provide comprehensive services.

Public services have also developed as a pragmatic response to requirements for service delivery.

Chapter Seven

The Role of Government

The influence of the 'radical right' extends beyond the advocacy of free economic markets discussed in chapter 5.[1] For Hayek, any expansion of the activity of government, however well-meaning it may be, represented a threat to personal freedom.[2] Nozick argues

> that a minimal state, limited to the narrow functions of protection against force, theft, fraud, enforcement of contracts and so on, is justified; that any more extensive state will violate people's rights not to be forced to do certain things, and is unjustified; and that the minimal state is inspiring as well as right.[3]

The primary objection to the idea of 'minimal state' is not that it does not exist in its purest form – nor does the welfare state – but that it represents something rather unpleasant. The sort of government that Nozick is arguing for is disengaged to the point of being immoral. Governments which have focused on law and defence while bypassing people's welfare – prominent at times in Latin America and North Africa – have generally been bad governments. It is not accidental that the world's richest countries – the countries in the OECD – are also the countries that spend most on welfare provision. Many of the world's newly formed democracies have not been formed because people think the role of government should be limited to defence, public order and the enforcement of contracts: they want, quite reasonably, the prosperity and the privileges of the West. Welfare is a fundamental part of that.

---

1. H. Glennerster and J. Midgley (eds.), 1991, The radical right and the welfare state, Brighton: Harvester Wheatsheaf.
2. F. Hayek, 1944, The road to serfdom, London: Routledge and Kegan Paul.
3. R. Nozick, 1974, Anarchy, state and utopia, Oxford: Blackwell, p. ix.

DEMOCRACY

Democracy is an obligingly flexible idea, and most countries in the world claim to be democratic in one sense or another. There are very different accounts of democracy. Some views of democracy are normative: democracy is a form of government that somehow reflects the will of the people or draws its authority from the people who are governed. The sort of idea that is referred to includes the sovereignty of the people, consent to government and the common good. Another class of accounts is institutional: democracy through democratic processes such as voting in elections, representation and political parties. For some, democracy is a normative ideal, expressing in some sense the idea that people are responsible for their own government. Then there are prescriptive approaches to political action: democracy is based on participation, account-ability, the representation of interests and 'deliberative' discussion.

The link between democracy and welfare may seem tenuous, especially if democracy is understood in an institutional sense. Some dictatorships have had a heavy commitment to public spending on pensions and benefits; there is a clear correlation between the size of spending on welfare and the size of the military;[4] and the 'checks and balances' associated with some sorts of constitutional government, such as the federal structures of the United States,[5] Australia[6] or Canada,[7] can act to create a series of 'veto points', reducing the likelihood that welfare legislation will be generally adopted. Despite that, Sen sees a deep connection between the mechanisms of democracy with the rights of the poorest people and the responsibilities of the state. There has never been a famine in a democracy.[8] Whether or not this is literally true – it all depends on how one defines democracy – there is something important to think about here. The reasons for it are obscure. It could happen that a poor majority vote themselves rights at the expense of a privileged few, but there are few places where that applies directly. It may be more important that democracy is based not on the votes of the majority, but the rights of minorities. For Sen, the com-bination of empowerment, property rights and public scrutiny by a free press act together to ensure that the position of poor people is protected.

---

4. H. Wilensky, 1975, The welfare state and equality, Berkeley: University of California Press.

5. J. Pressman and A. Wildavsky, 1984, Implementation, Berkeley: University of California Press.

6. F. Castles and J. Uhr, 2007, The Australian welfare state: has federalism made a difference? Australian Journal of Politics and History 53(10), 96–117.

7. K. Banting, 2004, Canada: nation-building in a federal welfare state, Bremen: Zentrum für Sozialpolitik.

8. A. Sen, 2001, Development as freedom, Oxford: Oxford University Press.

CITIZENSHIP AND THE POLITICAL COMMUNITY

A citizen is a member of a political community: citizenship is a set of rights associated with that status. The earliest conceptions of citizenship tended to emphasis the status – for example, the position of a Roman citizen – and the city-states of mediaeval Europe, which often referred to classical sources for their inspiration, tended to put the emphasis on issues of liberty and property, not on the provision of material resources. The history of citizenship, T. H. Marshall argued, shows a movement from the civil and political rights of the eighteenth and nineteenth centuries to the social and economic rights of the twentieth century.[9] Marshall's account looks initially plausible, but it mainly reflects the experience of a narrow group of countries; if one begins with welfare rather than civil rights, the link starts to look much less clear. The development of welfare provision can be traced through the development of cooperative, mutual and solidaristic arrangements, often in oppressive political regimes. In many countries, social rights preceded political ones.

There is some reason, nevertheless, to identify rights to welfare with citizenship. Where people enjoy the status of members of a community, their situation is not very different from the position of members of a club, and one of the purposes of clubs is to offer facilities to their members. "Government", wrote the conservative philosopher Edmund Burke, "is a contrivance of human wisdom to provide for human wants."[10] In the United States that is sometimes misunderstood as a 'socialist' principle, but it is a commonplace in every democracy – and even before democracy, political theorists argued that rulers had a general moral duty to do things for their people. *Salus populi suprema est lex,* wrote Cicero: the welfare of the people is the highest law. Marxists and neo-Marxists have often been critical of welfare, seeing it as a way of 'legitimising' the actions of capitalist governments.[11] If governments are providing their citizens with things they want and need, they are not pretending to be more legitimate: they are more legitimate.

From the other end of the political spectrum, 'libertarians' have argued that states cannot legitimately go beyond a minimal range of activities without infringing on the liberty of their citizens. The traditional American republican view of government, found in the *Federalist Papers,*[12] is that government is

---

9. T. Marshall, 1982, The right to welfare, London: Heinemann.

10. E. Burke, 1790, Reflections on the revolution in France, New York: Holt, Rinehart and Winston, 1959.

11. For example, J. Habermas, 1976, Legitimation crisis, London: Heinemann.

12. A. Hamilton, J. Madison and J. Jay, 1788, The Federalist papers, New York: Mentor.

dangerous and should be confined to a limited number of specified tasks. Hayek argued that

> the state, the embodiment of deliberately organized and consciously directed power, ought to be only a small part of the much richer organism which we call 'society', and that the former ought to provide merely a framework within which free (and therefore not 'consciously directed') collaboration of men has the maximum of scope.[13]

The core objection to this rests in the word 'merely'. Hayek supposes that actions which are permissible and desirable when they are undertaken by private enterprise on terms determined by an entrepreneur cease to be legitimate if they are implemented by an accountable government with specific authority to do them. There is a simple argument for governments going beyond the minimum – sponsoring athletics, organising public entertainments or floral displays (all activities, by the way, undertaken by Britain's supposedly market-oriented Conservative governments in recent times). Places which offer their people a wider range of pleasant activities are generally better places to live. If the activity is authorised, publicly accountable, subject to law, beneficial and does no wrong, why should governments not do it?

RESIDUAL AND INSTITUTIONAL PROVISION

Many welfare states developed outside the scope of government, and the role of government was consequently limited. Most governments, however, would accept at least a residual role. There are cases in which only government is left to act – that government becomes the provider of last resort. The English Poor Law, dating back to Elizabethan times, was supposed to confine its services to people who were destitute. It eventually developed into the basis of local government – covering issues in public health, medical care, education and housing – because in most cases there was no other organisation there to do so.

The general experience of most governments which take on the role of providing in the last resort is that they cannot hold to the boundaries. This is partly because of the pressure of other needs: the Poor Law developed health care in the nineteenth century because sickness was a major cause of destitution. It also reflects the difficulty of holding to the limits with any degree of equity (there were constant accusations that the minimal diets offered by the Poor Law were better than the virtual starvation of those who

---

13. F. Hayek, 1948, Individualism and economic order, Chicago: University of Chicago Press, p. 22.

lived without it[14]). As a general proposition, selective provision calls for an apparatus that can clearly distinguish those who are entitled from those who are not – a process that is burdensome, expensive and almost impossible to offer fairly. Personalised provision requires accurate assessment, huge amounts of information and rapidly responsive provision – demands that have sunk many overweening policies. Choice and competition call for duplication of resources and heavy administration. Universal services are often supposed to be more expensive than selective ones: that depends on what is being offered. Developing countries have been finding that basic, universal health care limited to covering a few conditions is much cheaper, easier to administer and more effective than trying to identify the poorest people individually. The Essential Health Care Packages promoted in Africa by the World Health Organization[15] have proved to be austere, strictly controllable, simple to administer and spectacularly effective. That runs counter, by the way, to the common assumption in the critical literature that universal provision must cost more.

This leads us to a different approach. Wilensky and Lebeaux referred to the welfare state as an 'institutional' model of welfare,[16] one in which certain "states of dependency" – Titmuss's term[17] – were accepted and provided for as a normal part of social interaction. Old age, sickness, unemployment and disability are conditions that any of us can undergo, that are made difficult because of the social arrangements we all have to live with and that we all need to be protected against. Once the state is committed to providing for the welfare of its citizens, the idea of defining arbitrary boundaries is hard to defend. If dependency and need are normal aspects of social relations, it is not surprising that a democratic political community should be organised to protect the interests of its members. It is rather more surprising when this does not happen.

COMPULSION AND CONTROL

In chapter 6, I considered a range of reasons why provision should be organised in terms of public service. Some of the arguments are practical, but

14. See J. Burnett, 1989, Plenty and want, London: Routledge; and I. Anstruther, 1984, The scandal of the Andover Workhouse, Stroud: Sutton Publishing.

15. World Bank, 1993, World development report 1993: investing in health, Washington, DC: World Bank; and see, for example, World Health Organisation, 2008, Essential health packages, Geneva: WHO.

16. H. Wilensky and C. Lebeaux, 1965, Industrial society and social welfare, New York: Free Press.

17. R. Titmuss, 1955, The social division of welfare, in Essays on 'the welfare state', London: Allen and Unwin, 1963.

those are not the only reasons why provision by the state might be a good idea. There are some things that governments do that cannot easily be done without their authority. One example is policing and other methods of imposing social control. The authority of the police depends in some countries on the authority of the legal system, in others on the authority of the government – but whatever the formalities, it is important that the police have legitimate authority. They are licensed to use limited force against citizens, and their role is distinctive. Prisons are another example. When governments 'privatise' services of this kind, they have to empower the private contractor to do what a public servant would do – but the private contractor must be no less accountable than the public one, which makes the distinction somewhat academic.

Another example of control is the use of compulsion to ensure public benefit. The use of compulsory purchase to build a road, a railway or an airport is an evident example in which the rights of individuals, in this case the property holder, are conditioned by the rights of the community. In parts of the United States, where the role of government is more heavily circumscribed, this is not always done by communities – it may be delegated to private enterprises under the doctrine of 'eminent domain'. That has the effect of exercising power with fewer safeguards and controls than apply in states in which government has a larger role. The use of compulsion has to be justified in terms of the exercise of legitimate authority, and in any state governed by the rule of law, all such actions have to be traceable to the authority of a legitimate institutional source – typically a constitution, a legislature or judicial precedent.

What happens, however, if a state wants to minimise its use of force? That position is commonly held in liberal democracies; there is a general sentiment that it is better for any force used by the state to be confined to a minimum, either by limiting its powers or by offering less intrusive alternatives. This has been called 'liberal paternalism'. So it is generally considered better for governments to offer citizens incentives than it is for them to issue orders; to ask for volunteers, rather than to conscript labour; to persuade or 'nudge' people than to instruct them.[18] (The principle seems to be that government intervention should be reduced, but there is an odd exception: market liberals generally oppose governments engaging in commercial enterprise, where they can seek to attract voluntary custom, because that is seen as distorting the market – so they demand that they tax people instead, an option which is then bitterly resented.) As governments come to exercise a wider range of

---

18. R. Thaler and C. Sunstein, 2008, Nudge, New Haven, CT: Yale University Press.

powers – regulating, steering, planning, bargaining, negotiating and so forth – so their influence is likely to extend.

WHAT GOVERNMENTS CAN DO AND WHAT THEY CAN'T

Once it has been established that governments may act, they are faced with an elaborate set of alternative things that they are actually able to do – as well as many that they can't. Because compulsory powers can be exercised in the final resort, there may be some reasonable suspicion that compliance depends on that compulsion, but there are many reasons why people comply with governmental directives, and it cannot be assumed that compulsion plays any direct part. The reason why people drive on the right or the left of the road is something that has been decided differently by different governments. There are certainly systems of enforcement to stop people doing the opposite, but there has to be some kind of rule or nothing will work, and the vast majority of drivers fall into line, not because there might be traffic police around ready to enforce the rules, but because it is not convenient or practical to do anything different.

Governments have a wide range of options open to them. They might use coercion – sanctions, criminal law, regulation – but they might equally use collaborative approaches, such as bargaining, negotiation, planning and partnership, and often those approaches are to be preferred. In the context of welfare, the choices are made more complex by the bewildering numbers of actors and participants in the process. In some spheres, governments have found that their powers are rather less than they might wish: this is particularly true in developing countries, where trans-national corporations and international organisations exercise considerable influence, but it is true of more developed countries too. Then governments need to decide whether their purpose is to do things themselves, through provision and purchasing, or whether they should be encouraging and persuading others to do things, through promotion and incentive structures. The model of governance which has gained ascendancy in the developing world – reflecting the influence of the IMF and the World Bank – is based on strategy formation, steering and partnership, rather than compulsion, direction and provision. Welfare broadens the range of mechanisms by which governments govern. Welfare provision offers mechanisms to persuade, promote or offer incentives, and consequently, where there are developed welfare services, government is better able to act proportionately within its legitimate sphere.

Some countries limit the power of governments to act through their constitutions, which define the limits of a government's authority and the proper scope of government actions. The main limitations on government, however, are not about powers. The most obvious restrictions are political (what will be accepted) and economic (what a government can afford to do balanced with all the other claims made of it). Less obviously, there are practical and administrative limitations to what can be done. Governments like to think they are in charge; some seem to think that they have a magic wand and have only to get the spell right and things will happen. If 'perfect administration' happens when a policy is performed exactly as planned, nothing is perfect. Some social policies have unexpectedly beneficial effects (a recent example might be the role of cash benefits for people on low incomes in allowing people to start businesses[19]); some have undesirable side-effects (such as the disadvantages experienced by children leaving residential care); but just about every policy has, to a greater or lesser degree, an 'implementation deficit' in which things do not happen quite as intended. Some problems, such as corruption or non-compliance, can frustrate the objectives of policy; some policies, such as the computerisation of information in health or social security, overreach the capacity of administrations to deliver. The neo-liberal critics of welfare have made a great deal out of 'government failure' as an objection to the provision of services.[20] Parts of that critique can be set aside: showing that governments have different priorities from the choices that are made through private markets is not an objection, but a basic part of the reason why governments might want to do things. Governments can fail because they are trying to do incompatible things: acting in ways that are open and accountable, limiting costs to a minimum and achieving the maximum effectiveness of policy are priorities that may well work to undermine each other.

WELFARE PLURALISM

Government is still only part of the welfare mix; there is considerable diversity in the provision of public services. Over the years, work in social policy has commonly distinguished four main sectors: public, private, voluntary and informal. The public sector refers to welfare provided by the state. The private sector includes both commercial arrangements, in which people pay for services in a market, and the work done by private firms, including occupational welfare and corporate social responsibility. The voluntary sector

---

19. J. Hanlon, A. Barrientos and D. Hulme, 2010, Just give money to the poor, Sterling, VA: Kumarian Press.
20. C. Wolf, 1978, A theory of non-market failure, Washington, DC: Rand Corporation; C. Winston, 2006, Government failure versus market failure, Washington, DC: Brookings.

mainly refers to independent non-profit activity, though there is a case for including social enterprise; equally, there is a case for considering mutuals (including mutual insurance) as distinct from either voluntary or commercial activities. And then there is the informal sector, the care given by families, friends and others. In many cases, particularly the care of older people and people with disabilities, this can dwarf the efforts made by government – to the extent that government services can only be planned as an adjunct to such care. While historically there have been societies with very limited organisation of the delivery of services, it is hard to imagine any society in the modern era in which some combination of the sectors would not be in play. Consider, for example, the organisation of pensions. In the vast majority of countries, there are three tiers of provision existing side by side: independent, market-based provisions which are made in recognition of a person's contribution, savings or work record; a general state scheme, which provides for most of the population; and a set of backup, safety-net measures for when the general scheme does not apply. Rein and Gunsteren have suggested that while there may be a general impression that pensions services are 'public' or 'private', the real issue is about the balance between them.[21]

In the wake of the New Right's assault on welfare, many existing arrangements have been dismantled to be replaced by some form of 'privatisation'. Privatisation is not a straightforward term, and in the context of the kinds of public service considered in this book, it has not necessarily led to the injection of market principles into the operation of services. Often it has meant the acquisition of assets and rights by private firms, but the contracts cover whole populations and include universal service obligations – a scale of operation that tends to preclude the diversity of approach or engagement of smaller-scale providers that market theory seems to promise. When the private sector starts to deliver public services, it is often represented as a way of bringing in the practices of the private sector – including competition, efficiency and know-how. Private sector providers just as often have to unlearn the things they know and to discover how to do them in a way that meets the standards and expectation of public service.

There are several reasons why this happens, but some of the simplest are 'functional', or determined by practical convenience. The basic arrangements that need to be made are collective ones, whether or not they are in private hands. The services providing social welfare are usually there for a reason. Some of those reasons have already been considered – humanitarianism, religious organisation and self-interest among them. One of the key arguments

---

21. H. Gunsteren and M. Rein, 1984, The dialectic of public and private pensions, Journal of Social Policy 14(2), 129–50.

for welfare states has been an argument for collective public provision, on a broader basis than can be done by smaller collective units. This is primarily a pragmatic explanation for public services, but over time it merges with a set of explanations that are thought of as being 'institutional' or established in society: the combination of long-standing practice, the existence of established organisational responsibilities and the acceptance of such arrangements as normal and desirable.

THE MAIN ARGUMENTS FOR WELFARE IN CHAPTER 7

Government is there to serve the interests of its citizens and to do things that people want to have done.

Democratic governments have stronger commitments to welfare, whether because they accept that citizens have rights, or simply because they are accountable to an electorate.

Government is a practical and legitimate option for the development of collective action.

Governments equally enhance their legitimacy by providing welfare. Some things that have to be done require appropriate legal authority which can only come from government. There is sometimes a case to use compulsion to ensure public benefit.

Government is the provider of last resort, which justifies residual provision; its role extends to institutional provision as it comes to accept further responsibilities for citizens' welfare.

Welfare broadens the range of mechanisms by which governments govern. Welfare provision offers mechanisms to persuade, promote or offer incentives, and consequently, where there are developed welfare services, government is better able to act proportionately within its legitimate sphere.

Chapter Eight

Welfare as a Way of Realising Other Values

The provision of welfare is often seen as an end in itself, but it may also be a means to other ends. The kinds of issue that the welfare states are concerned with – pensions, health care, schooling, benefits – are important for the ways that people live their lives. At the same time, these are also mechanisms, and mechanisms can be used in many ways, for good or ill. As mechanisms, they can be used for strictly instrumental purposes – to fund selected activities, to offer incentives, to regulate activity, to bargain for cooperation (a major element in European corporate governance) and so on. Equally, welfare provision can be pressed into the service of other political or social objectives. Governments can use social welfare services to increase equality or liberty – or, for that matter, to limit them. Both advocates and critics of the welfare state tend to see principles like social justice, equality and welfare as mutually supportive. The principles are discrete – capable of being distinguished – but the association has some justification: people who argue for social justice or equality argue for the provision of welfare, and people who argue against welfare tend to be dismissive of the other ideas.[1]

SOCIAL JUSTICE

The idea of 'social justice' has enjoyed a renaissance in recent years, largely following the publication of John Rawls's monumental work *A Theory of Justice*.[2] Rawls had preceded that book by a well-known article on 'Justice as

---

1. For example, F. Hayek, 1978, Law, legislation and liberty: the mirage of social justice, Chicago: University of Chicago Press; K. Joseph and J. Sumption, 1979, Equality, London: John Murray.
2. J. Rawls, 1971, A theory of justice, Oxford: Oxford University Press.

Fairness',[3] a title which captures something very important about justice – but in expanding the argument, much of his emphasis on fairness was lost.

There are two classic interpretations of justice, and Rawls sits uncomfortably between them. The first is the idea of justice put forward by Plato in *The Republic*.[4] Justice is about the moral organisation of the state: the things that are 'just are good and right'. The Platonic approach has no real limits: if justice includes whatever is good, almost anything can be said to be just. The UK Labour Party's Commission on Social Justice, in the 1990s, turned the report into a party manifesto of whatever seemed a good idea.[5] The Scottish Government's strategy for social justice suggests that communities should be pleasant places, and all children should be loved.[6] And so they should, but if things are going to be included only because they ought to be done, the argument for social justice comes to look a lot like an argument for doing anything that's good. If justice means everything, it means nothing.

The Platonic idea can mean whatever its proponents choose it to mean. For Rawls, justice is what people will consent to, and that a just solution is one they will accept if they do not otherwise know who will gain and who will lose from the processes they agree. The agreement is to be made under a 'veil of ignorance' – people do not agree or disagree because it reflects their own interests, because they do not know how things will actually turn out. What people agree ought to be good and right. This shifts the meaning of 'justice' towards a Platonic understanding of the concept. Rawls's method is intended to appeal to the sentiments of reasonable people, who he supposes will agree to the same principles that he does – but reasonable people can reasonably disagree.[7]

The other main model of justice comes from Aristotle. Justice, according to Aristotle, is about proportion.[8] Corrective justice calls for punishments that fit the crime; distributive justice calls for people to be treated according to their circumstances. David Miller reviews a range of ideas that might be seen as a principle of proportion: the recognition of established rights or status, contribution to society or merit and need.[9] If we think that the relevant criterion for justice is based on what people deserve, justice is likely to produce very

---

3. J. Rawls, 1958, Justice as fairness, Philosophical Review 67, 164–94.

4. Plato, The Republic, Book 1, p. 11.

5. Commission on Social Justice, 1994, Social justice: strategies for national renewal, Vintage, http://www.ippr.org/files/publications/pdf/commission-on-social-justice_final_2014.pdf.

6. Scottish Government, 2015, Creating a fairer Scotland, Edinburgh: Scottish Government.

7. See N. Daniels, 1975, Reading Rawls, Oxford: Blackwell.

8. Aristotle, Nichomachean Ethics, Book 5, in J. Thomson (ed.), 1953, The ethics of Aristotle, Harmondsworth: Penguin.

9. D. Miller, 1976, Social justice, Oxford: Oxford University Press.

unequal rights. If the relevant criterion is what people need, there is not much reason for large disparities in treatment.

The central principle at work across all these applications is a principle of consistency. If one accepts any general principle – liberty, rights, citizenship, human dignity or whatever – then proportionality will come into the way that the principle is interpreted and applied: any distribution has to be consistent with the relevant criteria. Nozick thinks that the only principles that matter are the established rights to property, and he condemns any idea that there can be a principle which might impose a different pattern on distribution of resources in society.[10] If we start with Nozick's assumptions, we might well come to the same conclusions – but there is no good reason to start there. Other principles, such as need, fairness or common humanity, are just as important as property rights. If the provision of welfare is proportionate to relevant factors, it can be difficult to justify the grosser inequalities or the deprivation of all resources to some: there is a reasonably strong case to say that people should have a common basic foundation.

Social justice in the Aristotelian sense is fundamentally a distributive concept. Rawls seems to be thinking about distribution when he talks about justice as fairness, and much of the substance of his arguments relates to a specific distributive idea, the 'difference principle'. Rawls believes that people will accept differences in outcomes if those differences lead to greater overall wealth for everyone. The difference principle is often accepted un-critically, but it is deeply misconceived. Inequality is corrosive. There is more than one way of deciding whether people are 'better off'. People can live in a developed first world country in which the riches of some sit side by side with a better life for most – better public health, roads, water supplies, energy, telecommunications and so on. At the same time, some, perhaps many, are excluded from the lifestyle, amenities and opportunities that are available to others. (This, Townsend argues, is what poverty means in contemporary societies.[11]) Some goods, Fred Hirsch argues, are 'positional'; the value of a private education or an exclusive residential estate is there because it is not available to others.[12] More generally, prices are relative; wherever resources are scarce, the people who will not be able to buy them will be those with less. Inequalities of purchasing power tend to price poor people out of essentials such as land or housing. This kind of exclusion is brought about by exactly the same process that leads to greater wealth through the difference principle. Wherever differences of this sort are allowed to take hold, reasonable people

---

10. R. Nozick, 1974, Anarchy, state and utopia, Oxford: Blackwell.

11. P. Townsend, 1979, Poverty in the United Kingdom, Harmondsworth: Penguin.

12. F. Hirsch, 1976, Social limits to growth, Cambridge, MA: Harvard University Press.

may well take the view, whatever Rawls says to the contrary, that they are unacceptable.

Philosophers sometimes distinguish 'thin' arguments, which are arguments based on simple, lean principles, from 'thick' ones, which are parcelled up with lots of detail. The 'thin' argument for social justice, the argument from consistency, is a strong one. The most powerful arguments against social justice come not from Nozick's superficial objection to 'patterned' responses, which simply fails to engage with the idea, but from the communitarian morality discussed in chapter 2. If each of us has special and distinctive responsibilities to other people, which cannot be generalised to other people, treating people consistently could not reflect the pattern of those responsibilities – it would be antisocial.

It is more difficult to make a 'thick' case in favour of social justice, or to prove that it is indeed relevant to decisions about distribution. However, there is still considerable scope for altering initial distributions – there is no good reason simply to accept that whatever has already happened is right. Welfare might compensate for disadvantage. It might seek to establish distribution according to need. It may seek to ensure basic minima for all humans. It may aim to distribute resources in accordance with people's rights. If justice is to be achieved through any kind of redistributive measure, then 'welfare', broadly understood, is likely to be the means through which that redistribution is achieved.

EQUALITY

Equality is not, as some critics would have it, about treating everyone the same: equality before the law does not mean that everyone gets seven years in prison. Saying that people are unequal means that some of them are disadvantaged, discriminated against or excluded. Where people are poor, that disadvantage extends into a range of social activities, including access to essential resources like food and shelter and life chances through education, communication, employment and more generally the ability to participate in society. The principle of equality is all about the removal of disadvantage.[13]

All welfare and all public services are redistributive: the people who benefit are not the same as the people who pay. Welfare is often assumed to be egalitarian. The pattern of redistribution may tend towards greater equality, but that is uncertain. Some welfare is egalitarian, some is not – and there have

13. See P. Spicker, 2006a, Liberty, equality, fraternity, Bristol: Policy Press.

been countries, such as apartheid South Africa, in which welfare was clearly organised on an inegalitarian basis. Some provision is solidly pro-poor: social housing, social assistance and welfare rights. Sometimes public provision favours people on higher incomes more than those on low incomes: libraries, railways, support for culture, higher education and (perhaps surprisingly) refuse tips. There are pension schemes that reward people according to their contributions: those are neutral, and in some cases they can be 'regressive', offering more to better-off contributors than they do to lower-paid people or those employed casually and temporarily. There are also some forms of provision that offer rather ambiguous benefits: prisons, policing and social work with families among them.

The difficulty of determining whether or not a service can be said to be 'egalitarian' is that there are many sorts of equality, and a service that supports people in one way might undermine them in another. A service that helps middle-class women be appointed to boardrooms helps address women's disadvantage, but it will not do much for people on low incomes. A policy to improve equality of opportunity will lead to some people gaining an advantage while others lose out. Rae identifies a series of conflicting types of equality. Some ideas look at individuals, some at 'blocs' like women or minority ethnic groups, some at 'segments' by comparing children or older people in a group, for example. Some forms of egalitarianism are concerned with prospects; some are concerned with means, such as income and wealth; some are concerned with outcomes. A policy that is egalitarian in one way might not lead to equality in another.[14]

There are many ways to understand equality. Equality of persons is the type of equality that tries to remove disadvantages of birth, race and gender; it should mean that people are treated as equals. Next there is equality of rights, a fuller, 'thicker' concept: the idea of human rights implies that everyone, regardless of their status, has rights which should not be denied to them. Those rights are usually taken to include life, liberty, access to justice and rights to own property; the Universal Declaration of Human Rights takes the principles further into rights to social security, a family life and basic resources.

Then there is the principle of citizenship. Citizenship is not intrinsically egalitarian, because some societies offer rights to citizens that they deny to migrants and non-citizens, but citizenship is the basis both of people's ability to command resources in a society and of empowering people in relation to political decisions. The equal treatment of citizens has been important to establish standards for women, people with learning disabilities and people with mental illness.

14. D. Rae, 1981, Equalities, Cambridge, MA: Harvard University Press.

Most of the patterns considered in these three categories are about process, rather than rights to welfare directly. A fourth understanding of equality is that it is about establishing minimum standards for everyone – in Tawney's words, seeking "to make accessible to all, irrespective of their income, occupation or social position, the conditions of civilisation which, in the absence of such measures, can only be enjoyed by the rich."[15] In my view, this is the sort of equality that matters most; it is also the concept of equality that is most strongly related to welfare. It implies minimum standards of food, health care, income, housing, education and so on – and 'minimum' does not mean the least provision possible, but a floor that is high enough to ensure that people have a good standard of living.

Fifth, there are arguments for equality of welfare – greater equality both of services and of outcomes. No-one has seriously argued for equality of income, but there are pressures for substantive equality in other fields. The literature on inequalities in health is concerned both that people from lower social classes are more ill and that they are liable to receive inferior services. There is an 'inverse care law'.[16] The expansion of higher education has been done partly to improve equality of opportunity, but it is no less important that higher education is seen as a major benefit in its own right.

Equality can be tied to the concept of justice – distribution according to citizenship, human rights or need all imply less inequality than there is at present. Even if the criteria lead to inequality, any principle of proportion begins with an initial presumption of equality: if there are no relevant differences, then people are treated as equals. Conversely, the idea of social justice can easily be harnessed to argue for a greater equality of incomes, resources or access to services. There may be an argument within the claim for social justice for extending welfare services that might make equality more attainable – for example, improving educational attainment, child care and employment. This, rather than Rawls's proposal of what people might assent to, is an idea of justice as fairness.

The link between equality and welfare is not solid; some welfare provision is unequal, and some is designed to make inequality greater. Having said that, if people have a level of services which offer them a good basic lifestyle and social protection which shields them from adverse conditions, then to that extent they will be more equal. Conversely, if people are more equal, whether that happens through citizenship, enhanced rights or access to basic systems of support, then their welfare will be improved.

---

15. R. Tawney, 1930, Equality, London: Allen and Unwin.
16. J. Tudor Hart, 1971, The inverse care law, in G. Smith, D. Dorling and M. Shaw (eds.), 2001, Poverty, inequality and health in Britain 1800–2000, Bristol: Policy Press.

FREEDOM

The relationship of freedom to welfare is complex, and more likely to be disputed than justice or equality. There are conflicting ideologies, which might be presented as an individual model and a social one. In the individual concept of freedom, a person is free if that person makes a choice and the choice is not subject to coercion. People do not stop being free if the action is impossible or frustrated: the test is what other people are doing to them. So, Isaiah Berlin argues, it is wrong to say that someone is not free because they are disabled or poor – those are just the circumstances in which people make their choices.[17]

This idea of individual freedom is limited in its scope, but even so it is difficult to realise without some kind of welfare provision. The first problem is that people whose choices are limited are vulnerable to coercion: closing off one option means little to someone with many choices and everything to someone with no other choice. The second is that the inability to make legitimate choices may be experienced as a form of coercion. Jeremy Waldron gives the powerful example of people who are homeless and unable legally to eat, sleep, drink or defecate, because there is nowhere they are permitted to do it legitimately.[18] The UN *Guiding Principles on Extreme Poverty* call on governments to 'repeal or reform any laws that criminalize life-sustaining activities in public places, such as sleeping, begging, eating or performing personal hygiene activities'.[19]

Social freedom is a broader, richer concept. Personal actions have to be understood in a social context; what people are able to do depends not just on themselves, but on everyone around them. Poverty implies an inability to participate in society – to do the sort of things that others in that society take for granted. In those circumstances, people are not free; to undertake autonomous action, they need to be empowered, whether that is through resources, rights or the structure of opportunity. And that implies, in turn, that people need to have a foundation of resources and opportunities so that they can exercise freedoms in a meaningful way.

It does not follow that every form of welfare provision enhances freedom. Some measures are restrictive; notoriously, some countries have used welfare as a means of oppression, such as the Soviet Union's abuse of psychiatric treatment. Welfare complements freedom when it empowers or promotes autonomy; it limits freedom when it indoctrinates or restricts. It should be

---

17. I. Berlin, 1969, Four essays on liberty, Oxford: Oxford University Press.

18. J. Waldron, 1997, Homelessness and the issue of freedom, in R. Goodin and P. Pettit (eds.), Contemporary political philosophy, Oxford: Blackwell.

19. United Nations, 2012, Guiding principles on extreme poverty and human rights, p. 17.

possible to dismiss, however, a common objection from libertarians, which is that the collective nature of welfare makes it intrinsically and necessarily coercive. Many forms of collective provision are voluntary; many more are empowering. Some, like health care and education, are capable of being coercive or empowering in equal measure; it is all a question of balance.

HUMAN DEVELOPMENT

The links between welfare and freedom can be seen as part of a broader constellation of issues. Welfare provision is more than social protection. The United States Constitution refers, similarly, to life, liberty and 'the pursuit of happiness'. The Universal Declaration of Human Rights refers to "the economic, social and cultural rights indispensable for [the individual's] dignity and the free development of his personality."[20]

This has often been translated into an argument that welfare can help with economic development. Internationally, the process by which economic development is being promoted has become a matter of governance rather than economics as such: countries supervised by the International Monetary Fund and the World Bank have been required to produce Poverty Reduction Strategy Papers, which (despite the name) are more concerned with economic development than with measures to deal with poverty. There has been increasing emphasis on the role of different kinds of provision in promoting economic development, and the 'Monterrey Consensus' marked an increasing emphasis on educational provision and health care as part of the process of development.[21] In many transitional and emerging economies, including all of Latin America, there has also been a marked extension of social assistance, typically in the form of 'Conditional Cash Transfers'. Hanlon and his colleagues argue that offering money to poor people has a major effect on local economies.

> Transfers can create a virtuous development cycle at the household and community level – and nationally. Families with an assured, though small, income begin to take small risks by investing in their future: buying better seeds to try to increase farm production, purchasing goods that can be resold locally, or even spending more time looking for better jobs. In impoverished communities, it is

---

20. United Nations, 1948, Universal declaration of human rights, Article 22.
21. United Nations, 2003, Monterrey consensus on financing for development, www.un.org/esa/ffd/monterrey/MonterreyConsensus.pdf.

hardly worth starting a business because none has money to buy. When they have a bit of extra income, most families spend the money locally, buying food, clothing and inputs. This stimulates the local economy, because local people sell more, earn more, and buy more from their neighbours, creating the rising spiral.[22]

Contemporary welfare states tend to complement economic performance, not least because policy choices are generally made with an eye to their economic implications. Richard Titmuss proposed an 'industrial achievement/performance' model of welfare in which the things that were done served the purposes of production.[23] The education system trains the workforce and provides child care; the health services keep the workforce healthy; social security is heavily geared to the demands of the labour market, facilitating the movement of some employees and the removal of others.

Development is about more than the economy, however, and increasingly international organisations refer to development in terms of 'Human Development'. When it published its first report on Human Development, the United Nations Development Programme put it this way:

> Human development is a process of enlarging people's choices. In principle, these choices can be infinite and change over time. But at all levels of development, the three essential ones are for people to lead a long and healthy life, to acquire knowledge and to have access to resources needed for a decent standard of living. If these essential choices are not available, many other opportunities remain inaccessible.
>
> But human development does not end there. Additional choices, highly valued by many people, range from political, economic and social freedom to opportunities for being creative and productive, and enjoying personal self-respect and guaranteed human rights.
>
> Human development has two sides: the formation of human capabilities – such as improved health, knowledge and skills – and the use people make of their acquired capabilities – for leisure, productive purposes or being active in cultural, social and political affairs.[24]

This is not about creating a particular type of human being; there is nothing here to say what the person is going to develop into. The idea of Human Development is based partly on a passive sense that people, to become people, must not be prevented by the lack of basic essentials – but it also takes an

---

22. J. Hanlon, A. Barrientos and D. Hulme, 2010, Just give money to the poor, Sterling, VA: Kumarian Press, pp. 6–7.
23. R. Titmuss, 1974, Social policy, London: Allen and Unwin.
24. United Nations, Human development report 1990, New York: United Nations, p. 10.

active view, that people have to develop capabilities to be able to flourish as people. The provision of welfare is central to both.

The Human Development Index used in UN reports takes three simple indicators: life expectancy, income and education. Those figures represent only a limited part of the issues – the Human Development reports are backed with a wide range of indicators on other topics – but they offer a useful spyhole from which a broader picture can be glimpsed. The countries which currently occupy the highest positions are Norway, Australia and Switzerland – not necessarily the countries with the largest public provision, but certainly countries with sophisticated, developed welfare systems.

THE MAIN ARGUMENTS FOR WELFARE IN CHAPTER 8

Welfare is an expression of moral values in itself, but it can also promote other core moral values.

Welfare promotes justice through fair, consistent distribution that is proportionate in its effects.

Welfare can promote equality both procedurally, through rights and access to opportunity, and more materially, in terms of citizenship, access to the conditions of civilization and the reduction of disadvantage in outcomes.

Welfare can promote freedom both in an individual and in a social sense.

Welfare advances human development to allow people to develop and use capabilities.

Chapter Nine

Policy for Society

The study of welfare is conventionally referred to as 'Social Policy'. For the most part, the term refers to a range of issues, policies and institutional arrangements (as it does in health care, pensions, social work, housing and so forth). The idea of 'social' policy does, however, seem to suggest something broader – policies for society, or 'societal' policy. There are social policies that are indeed policies for society, and some of them are considered in this chapter. It would be a mistake, however, to suppose that the welfare states are always concerned with such issues. On one hand, many policies concerned with social relationships have only a limited relationship to social welfare provision. Legal systems, for example, are deeply entwined with the definition and regulation of relationships, but mentions of the regulation of social relationships through tort, contract, equity and property law are hardly considered in social policy texts; the overlaps with family or criminal law are more likely to be recognised, but even in those cases the treatment is restricted. On the other hand, there are relatively few welfare policies which have a specific or direct focus on major social issues such as gender relations or ethnicity. It is easy enough to find connections between these issues and other policies, because these social conditions shape the circumstances in which social policies operate; the pervasive presence and influence of such issues implies that an evaluation of the impact of social policies may need to consider these issues to be fully understood. That is not, however, the same thing as saying the policies are 'about' those issues or that the connections relate to the policies' central purpose.

CHANGING SOCIAL STRUCTURES

Sociological analyses in general, and 'critical' social policy in particular, interpret the form of social relationships in terms of social structure. Inequalities of class, 'race', gender and caste are patterned through structures of power, material resources and access to opportunity. An emphasis on greater equality or disadvantage does not of itself imply a common pattern of policy – there are too many competing understandings of 'equality' for that – but it does signal a widely held view of policy. The welfare state, Esping-Andersen argues, "is not just a mechanism that intervenes in, and possibly corrects, the structure of inequality; it is, in its own right, a system of stratification. It is an active force in the ordering of social relations."[1] The Bismarckian system, for example, was used "to consolidate divisions among workers."[2] That could be taken to show that social policy reflects and reinforces social distinctions, rather than creating them; but it does seem to follow that if social policy can affect or change the pattern of social relationships, it ought also to be possible to use it deliberately to change those patterns. Ferge distinguishes social policy as it is commonly understood – the policy associated with social welfare services – from 'societal' or 'structural' policy, which attempts to change the structure of society. Structural policy "implies the project of deliberately changing the profile of a society, of altering basic human, social relations."[3]

Many of the policies concerned most directly with gender, race, class and minority rights are structural, part of a long-term plan to address social inequalities. The disadvantages that policy is addressed to are often deeply entrenched. Some patterns of disadvantage, such as caste, have been part of their societies for centuries; some are reinforced by long-standing practice and prejudice. Perhaps unsurprisingly, then, many structural policies fail to deliver. In the American 'War on Poverty', Quadagno writes, "the more traditional objectives of social policy to provide income stability and guarantee product markets became secondary to the grander struggle for racial justice."[4] Attempts to co-opt African Americans into the political process were not wholly unsuccessful, but their scope was limited and the inequalities have proved persistent. Education policy in the United Kingdom was for decades driven by class, but the early confidence that education could be an engine of equality was progressively eroded by evidence that it could not overcome the disadvantages associated with home background.[5] Several countries have complex policies in place to address the long-term disadvantage of indigenous peoples. The UN's blistering criticisms of Canadian policy point to the gap between aspiration and achievement:

---

1. G. Esping-Andersen, 1990, The three worlds of welfare capitalism, Cambridge: Polity, p. 23.
2. Esping-Andersen, 1990, p. 24.
3. Z. Ferge, 1979, A society in the making, Harmondsworth: Penguin, p. 55.
4. J. Quadagno, 1994, The color of welfare, New York: Oxford University Press, p. 28.
5. See, for example, M. Craft (ed.), 1970, Family, class and education, London: Longman.

The relationship of Canada with the indigenous peoples within its borders is governed by a well-developed legal framework and a number of policy initiatives that in many respects are protective of indigenous peoples' rights. . . . The numerous initiatives . . . have been insufficient. The well-being gap between aboriginal and non-aboriginal people in Canada has not narrowed over the past several years; treaty and aboriginal claims remain persistently unresolved; indigenous women and girls remain vulnerable to abuse; and overall there appear to be high levels of distrust among indigenous peoples towards the government at both the federal and provincial levels.[6]

Policies for gender equality face similar obstacles. The social policy of the European Union has put considerable emphasis on the rights of women, both in the workplace and beyond. 'Gender impact assessments' are undertaken to identify the ways that disadvantage comes about.[7] Walby argues, however, that the process has been hampered because the conventional division of policy areas does not deal with the way gender issues interconnect.[8] That point applies more generally. Well-made social policies are supposed to be specific, purposeful, targeted and designed to have predictable effects. The kinds of social issue which lead to structural inequalities tend, by contrast, to be general, interdependent and resistant to governance. There is a mismatch between what the advocates of structural policy hope to achieve and the mechanisms available to do it.

It is difficult to say how far social policies are able to shape the pattern or structure of social relationships deliberately. Even if welfare policies can be used as instruments to address deeper underlying issues, their effectiveness depends on the circumstances and issues to which they are addressed. Stratification and social division are part of the environment in which social policies operate. The importance of the big cross-cutting social issues for social policy, and the potential impact of policy on those relationships, is more something that needs to be taken account of, and the presence or absence of such impact is basic to many sociological critiques, especially in circumstances in which policy makers have failed to adequately consider the social dimensions of their actions. It is not self-evident that the existence of such relationships amounts to an argument for or against welfare provision.

---

6. United Nations Human Rights Council, 2014, Report of the special rapporteur on the rights of indigenous peoples James Anaya: the situation of indigenous peoples in Canada, Geneva: Office of the High Commissioner of Human Rights.

7. European Commission Directorate-General for Employment, Social Affairs and Inclusion, 1997, A guide to gender impact assessment, Luxembourg: European Communities, CE-16-98-788-EN-C.

8. S. Walby, 2004, The European Union and gender equality, Social Politics 11(10), 24–29.

SOCIAL POLICY AND SOCIETY

The basic proposition that welfare services can be used directly to shape social relationships may be open to question, but the idea that the issues are interrelated is hard to gainsay. That is in part true because aspects of social life, such as family and culture, are pervasive – it is difficult to see how welfare provision could not affect them or be affected by them. It is also true because welfare is not only a matter for the people who receive and use it: it has an immediate effect on the people around them. This could be interpreted in terms of interpersonal relationships, but more fundamentally it is an argument about the nature of society itself. Chapter 3 referred to the networks and groups that people belong to – families, communities, corporations and so on. A society is bound together through a complex series of overlapping, interlocking relationships. Social policy is bound, at least, to reflect those arrangements.

Welfare provision can be seen as an expression of moral relationships, and the terms in which welfare is discussed are often moral ones. In some societies, the discourse about welfare is distinctively social. The idea of the welfare state or *l'état-providence* is relatively rarely used in French debates, except perhaps as a way of dismissing the idea; there is a strong preference for using terms like 'solidarity' and 'insertion' instead. Solidarity is generally understood in most of Europe as a sense of mutual responsibility: "A firm and persevering determination to commit oneself to the common good, that is . . . the good of all and of each individual, because we are all really responsible for each other."[9] The French *Code de Sécurité Sociale* opens with the declaration that "Social Security is founded on the principle of national solidarity."[10] '*Insertion*', or social integration, is an aspect of social inclusion; people have to be 'inserted' into social networks. Integration refers to the attempt "to build the identity of a person around some community with which he is associated."[11]

The objective of 'social cohesion' is to ensure that these relationships are secure and lasting. Social cohesion might be interpreted in many different ways. The Council of Europe reviews a long series of alternative definitions of social cohesion, drawn from various sources. These include understandings of social cohesion based on social bonds, definitions based on shared values and a sense of belonging, collective action and cohesion based on harmonious coexistence:

---

9. Pope John Paul II, 1987, Sollicitudo rei socialis, Vatican: Catholic Church.

10. France: Code de Securité Sociale, 2015, Art L111-1.

11. K. Boulding, 1973, The boundaries of social policy, in W. D. Birrell, P. A. R. Hillyard, A. S. Murie and D. J. D. Roche (eds.), Social administration, Harmondsworth: Penguin, p. 192.

the promotion of stable, co-operative and sustainable communities

the ongoing process of developing a community of shared values, shared chal-
lenges and equal opportunities based on a sense of hope, trust and reciprocity

the extent to which people respond collectively to achieve their valued outcomes
and to deal with the economic, social, political or environmental stresses (positive or negative) that affect them.[12]

These are warm words, but the concept is potentially double-edged; cohesion can act as a fetter on individuals, a justification of inferior status for
women or a reason to exclude outsiders. Feudal societies and caste societies
are characterised by far-reaching duties without being counterbalanced by the
rights and freedoms that are also essential to contemporary life.

It may be that welfare provision is a way of conciliating people and avoiding potential conflict. At least as strong an argument can be made to suggest
that welfare incorporates aspects of social control. Provision for children,
for people with mental illness and for ex-offenders all attempt to promote
a degree of conformity with social norms. Education does much more than
equip children with access to culture, useful knowledge or even personal development; it introduces children to a pattern of life.[13] There is a case to say
that some other services – such as social work with families, employability
services and housing management – do as much, though in those cases the elements of control can be justified just as effectively by the impact that break-
ing norms has on other people. It can be difficult to work out whether social
control is a primary part of the activity of a service or whether some sort of
conditionality is imposed afterwards, as providers, funders and legislators
resile from the idea that people should receive benefits and services without
having specific obligations in return.

THE COMMON GOOD: THE WELFARE OF SOCIETY

Some of the ways that welfare states service 'societies' relate to society as a
whole and justify welfare in collectivist terms – an approach which brings us
back to the idea of a 'common good', first discussed in chapter 4. They rely

---

12. Council of Europe, 2005, Concerted development of social cohesion indicators: methodology
guide, Strasbourg: Council of Europe, pp. 24–26.
13. S. Bowles and H. Gintis, 1976, Schooling in capitalist America, London: Routledge and Kegan
Paul.

on the idea that something about the provision of welfare is useful for social purposes or detracts from it. Societies need to be maintained, and they need to reproduce themselves – making sure that the position of later generations is secure and the society continues to exist. The development of society for the future depends on doing work to safeguard future generations, equipping young people with skills, building roads, schools and public amenities, promoting culture and stewardship of the environment.

Titmuss once referred to society's collective "will to survive as an organic whole."[14] This way of thinking is not held in high regard nowadays. Society is too complicated and inchoate to have any purposes, and the idea that it has a collective will is preposterous. By contrast with many collective entities, a 'society' can seem remote. A society is more than a group; it is a meta-group, a collection of such entities or a network of networks. The defence of a country, the maintenance of its workforce and the development of its culture are all collective interests; for the same reason, they are actions for a common good, even if they may not necessarily be in the interests of every person.

The idea of 'social investment' can be seen as another way of expressing this. On the face of the matter, it is an extension of the principle of human development, considered in the previous chapter; societies are storing up assets for the future in the form of 'human capital'. (This is an old idea: Pigou argued for investment in human capital in the 1920s.[15]) Education is the paradigmatic social investment: spending on education prepares future generations for a role in society. For the World Bank, social protection is a way of maintaining the assets that society has and investing in the future: it is "a collection of measures to improve or protect human capital, ranging from labor market interventions and publicly mandated unemployment or old-age insurance to targeted income support."[16] A similar case has been made for the expansion of 'social capital', in terms of the capacity of communities to provide for themselves. Either might be justified in its own right as a way of addressing inequalities, but both can also be seen as a means of providing for the maintenance and development of society as a whole. It is difficult to evaluate the arguments for social investment, because it is difficult to collect and evaluate consistent data over a long period of time or to show what kind of return on investment a country might expect. The time scales are too long and the influences are too complex. But the arguments appeal intuitively – it makes sense to say that what is done now will have an effect on what happens much later, even if it is hard to prove.

---

14. R. Titmuss, 1955, The social division of welfare, in Essays on 'the welfare state', London: Allen and Unwin, 1963.

15. Cited in B. Nolan, 2013, What use is 'social investment'? Journal of European Social Policy 23(5), 459–68.

16. World Bank, 2009, Social protection, Washington, DC: World Bank.

There are dangers in the idea of the common good. A model that is based on consensus and the assumption of shared interests has the potential to lead to the suppression of minority interests and ways of living. However, it is possible to exaggerate the importance of individual differences, or of the preferences that people express; that happens in much of the economic theory which has been applied to these issues. Many patterns of behaviour are socialised. Old people have diverse problems, but by virtue of their age they share concerns about, for example, policies for retirement, pensions and the maintenance of health. Children require education, material stability and emotional support. Everyone is first a child, and most of us expect to become old; these concerns are likely to affect all of us in some way. Pensions, schooling and medical care are not universal truths of human nature. The ways in which the problems are defined and policies are formed to deal with them depend on the society in which they occur. People may differ in their choices or in their views as to how these issues are best dealt with, but the interests apply to these groups as a whole, and through them to every member of a society.

INDIVIDUAL AND SOCIAL OBJECTIVES

Some of the aims of social policies are meant to affect individuals and some are intended more broadly to benefit society, or at least parts of it. Welfare can be used to meet needs, to remedy disadvantage, to maintain circumstances, to invest in the future and so on, but it should not be assumed that those terms apply only to individuals. Table 9.1 is taken from my earlier work.[17] Social policy might be introduced to meet individual needs, but it might also be intended to promote the welfare of the whole society, for example through economic development. It may be used to address individual disadvantage, for example in compensation for disability, but it might also be intended to promote equality or social justice. It may aim to develop the capacity of individuals, for example through education, but it may also promote social capital and the capacity of society, for example by investing in the future.

This may give the impression that social policy is supposed to be constructive and positive, but there are other issuers to consider. Some of the other terms in the table – division, punishment and social control – are not about benefitting people at all. It may seem surprising to suggest that welfare might be used to divide society, but welfare provision is not only used to do friendly and pleasant things. The Nazis used it to distinguish Aryans from others. The

---

17. P. Spicker, 1993b, *Poverty and social security*, London: Routledge.

Table 9.1   Aims Commonly Attributed to Social Welfare Provision

	Individual	*Collective*
Provision for needs	Humanitarian	Social welfare; economic development
Remedying disadvantage	Compensation; cure	Equality; social justice
Maintenance of social circumstances	Social protection	Reproduction
Development of potential	Development of individual capacities	Solidarity; integration; social investment
Changing behaviour	Rewards; incentives; treatment	Social control
The production of disadvantage	Punishment	Social division

South African government reinforced apartheid by having different social services for different races. And social control includes measures for disciplining people – sanctioning criminal behaviour, supervising offenders, limiting people's ability to have unconventional households (for example, through polygamy) and limiting the actions of people who claim benefits.

These are not all arguments for welfare – some of them can reasonably be taken to be arguments against. The key insight to draw from this is that welfare provision is not any one thing, and simple-minded praise or condemnation is never good enough.

THE MAIN ARGUMENTS FOR WELFARE IN CHAPTER 9

Welfare can be used for social investment, developing both human capital and social capital and helping society to continue into the future.

Welfare provision is used to achieve social objectives. It can be used to promote social cohesion, integration and solidarity.

Chapter Ten

Does Welfare Have Bad Consequences?

Governments ought to try to do things which make people's lives better – that is what they are there for – and avoid doing things that make their lives worse. That principle is not accepted universally, because there are 'libertarian' commentators out there who hold that governments should do nothing even if their inaction hurts people, but it is a good argument in its own right. The test is whether welfare provision does, in fact, make people's lives better.

Comparing policies in different welfare states typically works by looking at differences in influences and outcomes between different countries. Many claims made in academic research about the effects of welfare politics and provision are based on a set of analytical techniques intended to distinguish the influence of selected variables from a host of other factors. One might read, for example, that

- spending on welfare affects family stability and the marriage rate;[1]
- policies on employment, debt and support for long-term unemployment affect household indebtedness;[2]
- increased educational spending is associated with greater employment;[3]

---

1. M. Halla, J. Lackner and J. Scharler, 2013, Austrian study: does the welfare state destroy the family? Vienna: Forschungsinstitut zur Zukunft der Arbeit.
2. S. Angle and K. Heitzmann, 2015, Over-indebtedness in Europe, Journal of European Social Policy 25(3), 331–51.
3. F. Castles, 2011, Have thirty years of comparative public policy scholarship been focusing on the wrong question? Bremen: University of Bremen.

- the economy shrinks when government grows too large;[4]
- the effectiveness of population policy depends on the age of the first child;[5] or that
- favouring social protection for old age ('silver welfare') "has a strong negative impact on State Effectiveness, Poverty, Housing and Intergenerational Fairness, while having no impact on Health or Education."[6]

This kind of assertion is sometimes plausible, sometimes not, but studies like this are unavoidably suspect. There is always a complex tissue of interacting factors to consider. Policies cannot be considered in isolation; several factors might come together in unexpected ways and outcomes can be complex. There are potential problems with the statistical methods that are used to make the analyses: the techniques that analysts used are complex and sensitive and the data rarely conform to the assumptions that the methods call for. The data are ambiguous, values are missing and evidence is picked out because it happens to be available. People working in this field have to accept that they are using 'indicators' – signposts and pointers – rather than precise information. The numbers, Castles argues, allow us at best to run "a preliminary sorting process, informing us about combinations of variables which fit together to produce possible accounts."[7]

ECONOMIC OUTCOMES

It is often argued that welfare is in some way economically damaging – that the burden of welfare payments is intolerable, that it holds back the economy, that costs undermine competitiveness or that increasing demands make the situation unsustainable. In the neo-liberal narrative, public actions undermine and crowd out private ones. There is some evidence to show an apparently negative relationship between welfare spending and long-term economic growth. At first sight, figure 10.1 seems to bear out the view that there is a relationship: there is a visible downward slope.[8]

But there is a general case for scepticism about this sort of evidence, and this is no exception. The first point to make is that growth should not be expected to occur at uniform rates everywhere. The richer, better established

---

4. D. Mitchell, 2005, The impact of government spending on economic growth, Washington, DC: Heritage Foundation.

5. G. Pierrakos, D. Balourdos, D. Soulis, M. Sarris, J. Pateras, P. Skolarikos and A. Farfaras, 2014, Comparative analysis and evaluation of the effectiveness of demographic policies in EU countries (2009–2010), World Health and Population 15(1), 31–43.

6. C. Brancati, 2016, Measuring state effectiveness, London: International Longevity Centre.

7. F. Castles, 1998, Comparative public policy, Cheltenham: Elgar, p. 20.

8. Data from OECD, 2016, OECD. stat, http://stats.oecd.org/.

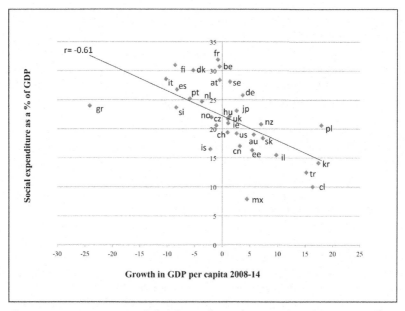

Figure 10.1. Recent growth has been slower in countries with more welfare provision.

economies are bigger, so proportionately they appear to grow more slowly even if they add income more rapidly; richer countries have shown a flattening off of growth, while the emerging economies have tended to grow fast. On the lower right, there are countries which are more recently developing – Mexico, Chile, Turkey and Korea. Second, growth has been influenced by a series of recent events that have no direct connection with welfare. Growth was strong up to 2008, and then there was a major financial crisis, which hit established economies harder. At the top there is the Euro-zone, with the outlier of Greece at the far left. These are countries which have some shared economic approaches, including restrictions on the role of government, rules obstructing expenditure on services and application of the same financial orthodoxy that justified structural adjustment in Africa. Reducing public expenditure tends to have a negative economic effect, because the change reduces the demand in the economy.[9] Then there are differences among countries, which the presentation in the graph glosses over: Germany, with higher social spending, has had better growth than the United Kingdom or the United States, Poland better than Hungary, Australia better than Canada. And

9. P. Krugman, 2012, Austerity and growth, again (wonkish), New York Times, 24 April; and see G. Zezza, 2012, The impact of fiscal austerity in the Eurozone, Review of Keynesian Economics 1(1), 37–54.

finally, there is a basic reservation to make: economic performance is about other things than social spending.

Keynesian economics treats expenditure on welfare not as a burden, but as an important set of levers to help manage the economy. Social spending can act as an economic regulator. This was seen, in the post-1945 settlement, as an important justification for welfare spending:

> Social security is sometimes described as a 'built-in' economic stabiliser. It has frequently been supported not only for the benefits it brings to individuals and their families, but also because it increases the stability of the economy. In Canada this was one of the reasons for the introduction of the family allowance system shortly after the end of the Second World War, as it was thought that there might soon be a severe trade depression . . . and that its severity would be mitigated by the regular payment of allowances for each dependent child in a family.[10]

When economic activity goes down, people become unemployed and benefit payments increase; when the activity increases, they become employed again and benefits payments reduce. This should act, in principle, to mitigate the effects of economic cycles. Putting money into an economy, or taking it out, has a ripple effect: in economics, this effect is understood in terms of a 'multiplier'. The calculation of multipliers is difficult, and the International Monetary Fund has recently revised its estimates because the size of the multiplier has an important effect on the accuracy of forecasts.[11] Underestimating the size of the multiplier implies underestimation both of the benefits of increased spending and the harm to the economy caused by cuts.

It is almost certainly true that cutting major services during a slump – the policy followed by governments in the 1920s and 1930s and repeated by advocates of 'austerity' more than eighty years later – is likely to exacerbate that slump. It is harder to say with confidence whether expanding services would mitigate the effect, because (with the main exception of Iceland) governments have not actually done it, but the position is at least plausible.[12] Probably the soundest economic strategy, in good and bad times alike, is to aim for regular, controlled growth and accommodation to circumstances.

There is at least a case to say that welfare shapes the ability of government to respond to changes in economic circumstances. The problem is that economic management calls for a measured response to changing circumstances, and it is exceedingly difficult at the same time to provide welfare in propor-

---

10. J. Richardson, 1960, Economic and financial aspects of social security, London: George Allen and Unwin, p. 215.

11. N. Batini, L. Eyraud, L. Forni and A. Weber, 2014, Fiscal multipliers, Washington, DC: International Monetary Fund.

12. See D. Stuckler and S. Basu, 2013, The body economic, Harmondsworth: Penguin, ch. 4.

tion to need or entitlements and to spend the right amount of money required for economic policy. Unemployment benefits may act counter-cyclically, but that is a small proportion of total expenditure. The amounts that governments spend on pensions, health care and education are not controllable over any economically convenient period.

The basic problem with attributing economic outcomes to welfare spending, either positive or negative, rests with the idea of expenditure in itself. A substantial part of what welfare states do isn't actually 'spent': it consists of 'transfer payments', in which money is moved from one set of people to another (and in particular, to pensioners), and they then choose whether to spend it in place of the people who might otherwise have done so. In principle, transfer payments are liable to be neutral in their effects – the same amount of money is in circulation before and after. That implies that a substantial proportion of welfare spending is unlikely to make much difference to the economy. If there are economic implications relating to the amount of money transferred, it has to be because the recipients may use the money differently from the contributors: they are probably more likely to spend it rather than to set it aside, and if they are poorer, they are more likely to spend it on essentials such as food and fuel.

The main social payments that are more than transfer payments are for medical care and education. It can be difficult to decipher the implications; the data are not necessarily comparable. Medical care potentially adds to national income, but it is accounted for differently in different countries. When a doctor treats a patient in a distinct commercial transaction, that adds formally to the total production and the income of a country. When it is done by a publicly funded health service, it doesn't. The National Health Service in the United Kingdom offers every citizen the equivalent value of medical insurance: that value does not feature in any accounts of personal income. Support for housing presents the same kind of problem. Some people live in subsidised housing; some countries use benefits to pay for housing; some have to pay for housing while others live without charge. In several developing countries, and even in some transitional economies, squatting is widespread; in others, poor people have to pay rent. To make the figures comparable, the World Bank has been considering whether it should impute rents to people who do not actually pay any.[13]

Most welfare spending is directed to older people, and that raises the further question whether this has specific economic implications. Pensioners are generally treated as a dependent population. They are unproductive economically, because they are removed from the labour market. In practice, pensions and other attendant costs such as health care for older people are paid out of

13. C. Balcazar, L. Ceriani, S. Olivieri and M. Ranzani, 2012, Rent imputation for welfare measurement, Washington, DC: World Bank Group.

current resources; those who remain productive have to pay for the elderly population. The amount spent on pensions is strongly correlated with expenditure on the welfare state, and that means that it is also apparently associated with slower growth – but by the same token, higher expenditure is associated with higher income, and higher levels of development are also indicative of higher productivity. There is no reason to suppose, then, that increasing numbers of pensioners are a drain on resources. The key issue is not that welfare consumes or extinguishes national income: it is that it is based on a transfer of income that some people do not think they should have to consent to. That is more a political issue than an economic one.

THE EFFECT ON INDIVIDUAL BEHAVIOUR

Many of the criticisms of social welfare provision focus on their effect on individual behaviour. For centuries, rich people have been criticising poor people for their demanding behaviour, lack of gratitude and repulsive habits. The criticisms are commonly based on a narrative in which welfare is introduced naively for noble purposes, but it falls into evil ways and is misused by those who would take advantage of it. This kind of criticism was prominent in the criticisms of charity during the Reformation, the association of the Old Poor Law with idleness and illegitimacy, the distinction of the deserving and undeserving poor in the late nineteenth century and the many condemnations of the disreputable poor – the 'submerged tenth', the lumpenproletariat, problem families and the underclass. This is from a report into poor relief in Ypres, written in 1531:

> Others that go begging, not because of their faith or because of their need, but to support their idleness, and cover their wickedness. They pretend to be poor. They live idly, and under the cloak of begging they craftily hide their laziness and mischief, to the great cost of the State.[14]

This is from an English pamphlet, published in 1752:

> When the Statute of Elizabeth relieving the Poor first took place, the Burthen was light and inconsiderable. Few applied for relief. It was a Shame and a Scandal for a person to throw himself on a parish . . . but the Sweets of Parish-Pay being once felt, more and more Persons soon put in for a share of it. One cried, he as much wanted, and might as well accept it, as another; the Shame grew less and less, and Numbers encouraged and countenanced one another.[15]

---

14. City of Ypres, 1531, Forma subventionis pauperum, in P. Spicker, 2010, The origins of modern welfare, Oxford: Peter Lang.

15. T. Alcock, 1752, Observations on the defects of the Poor Laws, London: Baldwin and Clements, pp. 16–17.

This is an anonymous critic, writing in 1835:

> Poverty will leave its impress upon all men, both as regards habits and manners, but it was left for the pauper system of England to show that it might be rendered available to the destruction of their feelings, and strike out of the machine of man the mainspring of his moral movements, namely – a sense of shame.[16]

There is some reason to think that the complaints are false. At the most general level, these arguments have been made for hundreds of years, and the gains in economic, social and human development over that time have improved ordinary people's lives immeasurably. It is hardly possible to argue that welfare provision has changed behaviour in the current generation if the same complaints were present in previous generations. At a much more detailed level, most of the contentions about dependency have been undermined by research into the problems. International studies of the dynamics of welfare have painted a very different picture of the extent to which people of working age become 'dependent' over long periods. People receiving benefits in Germany and the United Kingdom tend to move back and forth between different circumstances.[17] Many people experience rapid and unpredictable changes of fortune – a phenomenon which has given rise to arguments that there is a 'precariat' class.[18] Prospects for employment and earning vary with the state of the economy. Over a longer period of time, people are likely to undergo major changes due to their age and opportunities – income tends to rise when people first form a household, to fall when women move to child care and to fall more markedly in older age. All this makes it more unlikely that patterns of long-term dependency will continue throughout a person's lifetime, let alone that this will be replicated in future generations – one recent study commented that trying to find even a single family that had been dependent over three generations was like 'the search for the Yeti'.[19] Longitudinal studies have found both that people's prospects are not fixed – education, the economy and partnering all make a marked difference[20] – and that, over very long periods of time, it becomes almost impossible to predict who will and who will not experience poverty.

---

16. T. Wontner, 1835, Abolition of pauperism, London: Steill, p. 4.
17. P. Buhr and S. Leibfried, 1995, What a difference a day makes, in G. Room (ed.), Beyond the threshold, Bristol: Policy Press; L. Leisering and R. Walker (eds.), 1998, The dynamics of modern society, Bristol: Policy Press.
18. G. Standing, 2014, The precariat, New York: Bloomsbury.
19. R. Macdonald, T. Shildrick and A. Furlong, 2013, In search of 'intergenerational cultures of worklessness': hunting the yeti and shooting zombies, Critical Social Policy 26 September.
20. For example, A. Atkinson, A. Maynard and C. Trinder, 1983, Parents and children, London: Heinemann; M. Brown and N. Madge, 1982, Despite the welfare state, London: Heinemann; I. Kolvin, F. J. W. Miller, D. M. Scott, S. R. M. Gatzanis and M. Fleeting, 1990, Continuities of deprivation?: the Newcastle 1000 family study, Aldershot: Avebury.

Most of the arguments about the evil consequences of welfare rely on sweeping generalisations about the impact of welfare states. The evidence does not bear out the negative accounts. It is just not true that spending has spiralled out of control, that welfare breeds dependency or that people stay on benefits for generations. The accusations that welfare have encouraged dependency or alienation from conventional morality have been made repeatedly, which does not make them any more convincing. If they were true, there should be more social problems, more violence and more disorder in countries which have more generous welfare systems. There isn't. There is probably a case on the other side to say that there is less crime in circumstances in which people's lifestyles are more equal,[21] and that more developed welfare systems do offer access to the conditions of civilisation – but that is as far as the evidence goes.

GOOD WELFARE AND BAD WELFARE

It is not an argument for welfare to assume that it does nothing but good any more than it is an argument against it to assume that it does nothing but bad. The limitations of the evidential base should be enough to make people pause before they generalise about the consequences of welfare, but that is not the only problem. A much more fundamental objection is that it is questionable whether any evidence could ever prove either position beyond doubt. There is no single policy or set of policies that defines a 'welfare state', and what there is cannot be separated from the constellation of economic, social and political circumstances in which welfare states operate.

There is a much better case for saying specific welfare policies might have specific effects, or at least help to achieve certain outcomes. Castles is particularly critical of the tendency in comparative studies to focus on general expenditure on welfare, rather than what is being bought with the money.[22] Governments need to test whatever they are doing to see that the policy is doing what it is supposed to. Some policies are more effective, some are less so.

Effective policies are not necessarily good or bad. A policy based on good intentions can be implemented clumsily, and a bad policy can be carried out with ruthless efficiency. What makes a policy worth doing depends on the arguments in chapter 2 – the evaluation may be based on outcomes, but it may also be a matter of principle. Some policies are morally objectionable, even if they seem by some tests to work – for example, the methods used by Stalin to advance

---

21. R. Wilkinson and K. Pickett, 2009, The spirit level, London: Allen Lane.
22. Castles, 2011.

industrialisation. Some policies may seem not to work, but they can still be defended morally – taking abused children into places of safety. The measures that governments take cannot be considered only in terms of their impacts.

The fundamental weakness of many neo-liberal and conservative critiques of the welfare state lies not so much in the lack of conclusive evidence, because the evidence on the other side is not always conclusive either, but in their failure to distinguish good policies from bad ones. Humanitarian action by government, such as international aid or support for the poor, is characterised as naive and destructive; policies which promote autonomy and dignity, such as decent housing or health care, are assailed as attacks on individual freedom; the general run of welfare policies, such as pensions and unemployment insurance, are dismissed as illegitimate – governments do not have the right to introduce them, or even to do what a voluntary association might do in their place. These arguments lead nowhere. Once it is accepted that humanitarian action is a good thing, that individuals have needs or that governments can legitimately do things, the objectors offer no guidance about what to do next or how to do it.

Conversely, however, arguments for welfare have to take into account the possibility that things can and do go wrong. Any argument that begins with the proposition that there will be some kind of welfare provision needs to move on to identify what sort of welfare provision it will be. Any argument based on the use of welfare as a mechanism or instrument has to recognise that instruments can be used for bad things as well as good ones. In every case, it is important to ensure that welfare provision always acts within the scope of public authority, that it is open to public scrutiny and that when it goes wrong – as it will – it can be set right. That is not an argument against welfare; it is an argument for doing it better.

THE MAIN ARGUMENTS FOR WELFARE IN CHAPTER 10

Welfare provision is used to achieve economic and social ends. It is a tool of economic management; it can be, and is being, used to promote economic development. It might also be used to shape individual behaviour.

Most generic criticisms of the effects of welfare are ill-founded. Generalised claims that welfare leads to bad behaviour, economic failure or inter-generational dependency are not based on solid evidence.

Chapter Eleven

Why Welfare?

This short book has presented twenty-six of the principal reasons for the provision of welfare.

A. Welfare is the right thing to do if

- it has good consequences,
- it is consistent with general moral rules, such as human rights or the principles of major religions,
- it is done in recognition of specific obligations, or
- it is the sort of thing done by good people.

However, it cannot be assumed that welfare is good or bad in itself. It all depends on what the provision is and what it is doing.

B. It is good to do things for other people, whether this is done out of

- benevolence, altruism or humanitarianism, or
- a sense of social responsibility, duty or reciprocity.

C. Sometimes we feel, morally, that

- something must be done,
- people are in need, or that
- state or social organisations have to take action.

D. People have a range of rights to welfare:

- particular rights gained from interaction, exchange and contract,
- rights of citizenship, and
- human rights.

E. Welfare serves people's interests.

- People who are self-interested tend to choose to have welfare.
- People make collective arrangements with others for their mutual benefit and to further their common and shared interests. If the choices which lead to them being set up are legitimate, so are the arrangements.

F. Welfare furthers the common good:

- the interests which people have in common, and
- the interests they share as members of a community or members of a society.

G. There are limits to markets.

- Markets sometimes 'fail', in the sense that they cannot work adequately.
- The advantages claimed for markets cannot consistently be realised, because many of the situations that welfare provision has to deal with are different from the conventional representation of production and economic exchange. The demand for services cannot be met consistently and effectively through commodification and exchange.
- There would be gaps even if markets were to function perfectly. Markets cannot do everything. Some other arrangement has to be made.

H. Some universal standards are needed for people to function as individuals, to live with dignity and to make it possible to thrive and make choices.

I. There is also a need to protect some people.

J. Welfare needs to be delivered through public services, which cannot operate as businesses do.

- Public services have developed to deliver services in ways that are compatible with public policy. Beginning with policy requires services to be directed to meet aims effectively and be accountable in those terms.

- To achieve the aims of policy, and because they cannot be funded by payment at the point of consumption, public services have to operate as a trust.

K. Public services may be developed

- to deliver social goods,
- to ensure minimum standards,
- to develop services which users could not realistically pay for in their own right, or
- to provide comprehensive services.

L. Public services have also developed as a pragmatic response to requirements for service delivery.

M. Government is there to serve the interests of its citizens and to do things that people want to have done.

N. Democratic governments have stronger commitments to welfare

- if they accept that citizens have rights or
- if they are accountable to an electorate.

O. Government is a practical and legitimate option for the development of collective action. Equally, governments enhance their legitimacy by providing welfare.

P. Government depends on legal authority, and welfare may rely on the exercise of such authority.

- Some things that have to be done require appropriate legal authority which can only come from government.
- There is sometimes a case to use compulsion to ensure public benefit.

Q. Welfare broadens the range of mechanisms by which governments govern. Welfare provision offers mechanisms to persuade, promote or offer incentives. Consequently, where there are developed welfare services, government is better able to act proportionately within its legitimate sphere.

R. Government is the provider of last resort, which justifies residual provision; its role extends to institutional provision as it comes to accept further responsibilities for citizens' welfare.

S. Welfare is an expression of moral values in itself, but it can also promote other core moral values.

T. Welfare can promote social justice through a fair, consistent distribution that is proportionate in its effects.

U. Welfare can promote equality both procedurally and materially:

- procedurally, through
- rights
- access to opportunity, and
- materially, in terms of
- citizenship,
- access to the conditions of civilization, and
- the reduction of disadvantage in outcomes.

V. Welfare can promote freedom

- in an individual sense, through autonomy and personal choice, and
- in a social sense, through empowerment and collective capacity.

It advances human development, allowing people to develop and realise their capabilities.

W. Welfare can be used for social investment, developing both human capital and social capital and helping society to continue into the future.

X. Welfare provision is used to achieve economic ends.

- It is a tool of economic management;
- It is used to promote economic development.

Y. Welfare provision is used to achieve social objectives, including

- social cohesion,
- integration and
- solidarity.
- Welfare is an investment for the future;
- it might also be used to shape individual behaviour.

Z. Most generic criticisms of the effects of welfare are ill-founded. Generalised claims that welfare leads to bad behaviour, economic failure or intergenerational dependency are not based on solid evidence.

Bibliography

Alcock, T. 1752. Observations on the defects of the Poor Laws. London: Baldwin and Clements.

Anderton, A. 1997. Economics. Ormskirk: Causeway Press.

Angle, S., and K. Heitzmann. 2015. Over-indebtedness in Europe. Journal of European Social Policy 25(3), 331–51.

Anstruther, I. 1984. The scandal of the Andover Workhouse. Stroud: Sutton Publishing.

Aristotle. Nichomachean ethics. In Thomson, J. (ed.), The ethics of Aristotle. Harmondsworth: Penguin, 1953

Atkinson, A. B. 1995. The welfare state and economic performance. In Incomes and the welfare state. Cambridge: Cambridge University Press.

Atkinson, A., A. Maynard and C. Trinder. 1983. Parents and children. London: Heinemann.

Balcazar, C., L. Ceriani, S. Olivieri and M. Ranzani. 2012. Rent imputation for welfare measurement. Washington, DC: World Bank Group.

Baldwin, P. 1990. The politics of social solidarity. Cambridge: Cambridge University Press.

Banting, K. 2004. Canada: nation-building in a federal welfare state. Bremen: Zentrum für Sozialpolitik.

Barry, N. 1987. The new right. Beckenham: Croom Helm.

Batini, N., L. Eyraud, L. Forni and A. Weber. 2014. Fiscal multipliers. Washington, DC: International Monetary Fund.

Battle, K. 1998. Transformation: Canadian social policy since 1985. Social Policy and Administration 32(4), 321–40.

BBC. 2015. Snakebite antidote is running out. http://www.bbc.co.uk/news/health-34176581.

Beck, U. 1992. Risk society. London: Sage.

Begg, I., F. Mushovel and R. Niblett. 2015. The welfare state in Europe. London: Chatham House.

Bentham, J. 1789. An introduction to the principles of morals and legislation. In M. Warnock (ed.), Utilitarianism. Glasgow: Collins, 1962.

Berlin, I. 1969. Four essays on liberty. Oxford: Oxford University Press.

Boulding, K. 1973. The boundaries of social policy. In W. D. Birrell, P. A. R. Hillyard, A. S. Murie and D. J. D. Roche (eds.), Social administration. Harmondsworth: Penguin.

Bowles, S., and H. Gintis. 1976. Schooling in capitalist America. London: Routledge and Kegan Paul.

Boyne, G. 2002. Public and private management: what's the difference? Journal of Management Studies 39(1), 97–122.

Brancati, C. 2016. Measuring state effectiveness. London: International Longevity Centre.

Briggs, A. 1961. The welfare state in historical perspective. European Journal of Sociology 2, 221–58.

Brodman, J. 2009. Charity and religion in medieval Europe. Washington, DC: Catholic University of America Press.

Brown, M., and N. Madge. 1982. Despite the welfare state. London: Heinemann.

Buhr, P., and S. Leibfried. 1995. What a difference a day makes. In G. Room (ed.), Beyond the threshold. Bristol: Policy Press.

Burke, E. 1790. Reflections on the revolution in France. New York: Holt, Rinehart and Winston, 1959.

Burnett, J. 1989. Plenty and want. London: Routledge.

Cass, B., and J. Freeland. 1994. Social security and full employment in Australia. In J. Hills, J. Ditch and H. Glennerster (eds.), Beveridge and social security. Oxford: Clarendon Press.

Castles, F. 1998. Comparative public policy. Cheltenham: Elgar.

_____. 2008. What welfare states do. Journal of Social Policy 38(1), 45–62.

_____. 2011. Have thirty years of comparative public policy scholarship been focusing on the wrong question? Bremen: University of Bremen. http://hdl.handle .net/10419/52222.

Castles, F., and J. Uhr. 2007. The Australian welfare state: has federalism made a difference? Australian Journal of Politics and History 53(10), 96–117.

Clasen, J., and D. Clegg. 2007. Levels and levers of conditionality. In J. Clasen and N. Siegel (eds.), Investigating welfare state change. Cheltenham: Edward Elgar.

Cmd 6404. 1942. Social insurance and allied services. London: HMSO.

Commission on Social Justice. 1994. Social justice: strategies for national renewal. Vintage, http://www.ippr.org/files/publications/pdf/commission-on-social-justice _final_2014.pdf.

Cooper, M., and A. Culyer. 1968. The price of blood. London: Institute of Economic Affairs.

Council of Europe. 2005. Concerted development of social cohesion indicators: methodology guide. Strasbourg: Council of Europe.

Craft, M. (ed.). 1970. Family, class and education. London: Longman.

Daniels, N. 1975. Reading Rawls. Oxford: Blackwell.

d'Entrèves, A. 1970. Natural law. London: Hutchinson.

Ditch, J. 1999. Full circle: a second coming for social assistance? In J. Clasen (ed.), Comparative social policy. Oxford: Blackwell.

Dwyer, P. 2004. Creeping conditionality in the UK. Canadian Journal of Sociology 29(4), 265–87.

Economist. 2013. The Merkel plan. http://www.economist.com/news/special-report/21579144-germanys-vision-europe-all-about-making-continent-more -competitive-merkel.

Esping-Andersen, G. 1990. The three worlds of welfare capitalism. Cambridge: Polity.

European Commission Directorate-General for Employment, Social Affairs and Inclusion. 1997. A guide to gender impact assessment. Luxembourg: European Communities, CE-16-98-788-EN-C.

European Observatory of Working Life. 2011. Social protection. http://www .eurofound.europa.eu/observatories/eurwork/industrial-relations-dictionary/ social-protection.

Ferge, Z. 1979. A society in the making. Harmondsworth: Penguin.

France: Code de Securité Sociale. 2015. Art L111-1. https://www.legifrance.gouv.fr/.

Friedman, M. 1962. Capitalism and freedom. Chicago: University of Chicago Press.

Glennerster, H., and J. Midgley (eds.). 1991. The radical right and the welfare state. Brighton: Harvester Wheatsheaf.

Gordon, D., L. Adelman, K. Ashworth, J. Bradshaw, R. Levitas, S. Middleton, C. Pantazis, D. Patisos, S. Payne Townsend and J. Williams. 1999. Poverty and social exclusion in Britain. York: Joseph Rowntree Foundation.

Gouldner, A. 1960. The norm of reciprocity. American Sociological Review 25(2), 161–77.

Green, D. 1993. Reinventing civil society. London: Civitas.

Griffin, J. 1986. Well-being. Oxford: Oxford University Press.

Gunsteren, H., and M. Rein. 1984. The dialectic of public and private pensions. Journal of Social Policy 14(2), 129–50.

Habermas, J. 1976. Legitimation crisis. London: Heinemann.

Halla, M., J. Lackner and J. Scharler. 2013. Austrian study: does the welfare state destroy the family? Vienna: Forschungsinstitut zur Zukunft der Arbeit. http://ftp .iza.org/dp7210.pdf.

Hamilton, A., J. Madison and J. Jay. 1788. The Federalist papers. New York: Mentor.

Hanlon, J., A. Barrientos and D. Hulme. 2010. Just give money to the poor. Sterling, VA: Kumarian Press.

Hardin, G. 1968. The tragedy of the commons. In R. Kuenne (ed.), Readings in social welfare. Oxford: Blackwell, 2000.

Hayek, F. 1944. The road to serfdom. London: Routledge and Kegan Paul.

_____. 1948. Individualism and economic order. Chicago: University of Chicago Press.

_____ 1960. The constitution of liberty. London: Routledge and Kegan Paul.

_____. 1978. Law, legislation and liberty: the mirage of social justice. Chicago: University of Chicago Press.

Heyneman, S. (ed.). 2004. Islam and social policy. Nashville: Vanderbilt University Press.

Hirsch, F. 1976. Social limits to growth. Cambridge, MA: Harvard University Press.

HM Treasury. N.d. Green Book. http://www.hm-treasury.gov.uk/d/green_book_complete.pdf.

House of Commons Work and Pensions Committee. 2013. Can the work programme work for all user groups? House of Commons.

Jordan, B. 1996. A theory of poverty and social exclusion. Brighton: Polity.

Joseph, K., and J. Sumption. 1979. Equality. London: John Murray.

King, D. 1987. The new right. Basingstoke: Macmillan.

Klass, G. 1985. Explaining America and the welfare state. British Journal of Political Science 15, 427–50.

Kolvin, I., F. J. W. Miller, D. M. Scott, S. R. M. Gatzanis and M. Fleeting. 1990. Continuities of deprivation?: the Newcastle 1000 family study. Aldershot: Avebury.

Kotb, S. 1970. Social justice in Islam. New York: Octagon Books.

Kovner, A., and J. Knickman. 2013. Jonas and Kovner's health care delivery in the United States. New York: Springer.

Krugman, P. 2012. Austerity and growth, again (wonkish). New York Times, 24 April, http://krugman.blogs.nytimes.com/2012/04/24/austerity-and-growth-again-wonkish/.

Latané, B., and J. Darley. 1970. The unresponsive bystander. New York: Appleton-Century-Crofts.

Lawrence, F. 2013. Private health contractor's staff told to cut 999 calls to meet targets. The Guardian, 23 January, http://www.guardian.co.uk/society/2013/jan/23/private-health-contractor-999-calls.

Law Report: In the matter of Capita Translation and Interpreting Limited [2015] EWFC 5. http://www.familylawweek.co.uk/site.aspx?i=ed143010.

Leisering, L., and R. Walker (eds.). 1998. The dynamics of modern society. Bristol: Policy Press.

Locke, J. 1690? Two treatises of civil government, P. Laslett (ed.). New York: Mentor, 1965.

Maccallum, G. 1967. Negative and positive freedom. Philosophical Review 76, 312–34.

Macdonald, R., T. Shildrick and A. Furlong. 2013. In search of 'intergenerational cultures of worklessness': hunting the yeti and shooting zombies. Critical Social Policy 26 September.

MacIntyre, A. 1981. After virtue. London: Duckworth.

Marshall, T. 1982. The right to welfare. London: Heinemann.

Mead, L. 1992. The new politics of poverty. New York: Basic Books.

Mill, J. S. 1861 [1962]. Utilitarianism, in M. Warnock (ed.), Utilitarianism. Glasgow: Collins, 1962.

Miller, D. 1976. Social justice. Oxford: Oxford University Press.

Mitchell, D. 2005. The impact of government spending on economic growth. Washington, DC: Heritage Foundation.

Mohan, G., E. Brown, B. Milward and A. Zack-Williams. 2000. Structural adjustment. London: Routledge.

Mullard, M., and P. Spicker. 1998. Social policy in a changing society. London: Routledge.

Murray, C. 1984. Losing ground. New York: Basic Books.

Myles, J. 1998. How to design a 'liberal' welfare state: a comparison of Canada and the United States. Social Policy and Administration 32(4), 341–64.

Needham, C. 2011. Personalising public services. Bristol: Policy Press.

Nickerson, R. 1998. Confirmation bias. Review of General Psychology 2(2), 175–220.

Niemietz, K. 2015. What are we afraid of? Universal healthcare in market-oriented health systems. London: Institute for Economic Affairs.

Nolan, B. 2013. What use is 'social investment'? Journal of European Social Policy 23(5), 459–68.

Nozick, R. 1974. Anarchy, state and utopia. Oxford: Blackwell.

Oakeshott, M. 1975. The vocabulary of a modern European state. Political Studies 23(2–3), 319–41.

OECD. 2016. OECD.stat. http://stats.oecd.org/.

Olson, M. 1971. The logic of collective action. Cambridge, MA: Harvard University Press.

Osborne, S., Z. Radnor and G. Nasi. 2013. A new theory for public service management? American Review of Public Administration 43(2), 135–58.

Palier, B., and G. Bonoli. 1995. Entre Bismarck et Beveridge. Revue Française de Science Politique 45(4), 668–99.

Paton, H. 1948. The moral law: Kant's groundwork of the metaphysics of morals. London: Hutchinson.

Pfohl, S. 2003. The 'discovery' of child abuse, in P. Conrad and V. Leiter (eds.), Health and health care as social problems. Lanham, MD: Rowman & Littlefield.

Pierrakos, G., D. Balourdos, D. Soulis, M. Sarris, J. Pateras, P. Skolarikos and A. Farfaras. 2014. Comparative analysis and evaluation of the effectiveness of demographic policies in EU countries (2009–2010). World Health and Population 15(1), 31–43, http://www.ncbi.nlm.nih.gov/pubmed/24702764.

Plato. The Republic. http://classics.mit.edu/Plato/republic.html.

Ploug, N., and J. Kvist (eds.). 1994. Recent trends in cash benefits in Europe. Copenhagen: Danish National Institute of Social Research.

Pope John Paul II. 1987. Sollicitudo rei socialis. Vatican: Catholic Church.

Poteete, A., M. Janssen and E. Ostrom. 2010. Working together. Princeton, NJ: Princeton University Press.

Pressman, J., and A. Wildavsky. 1984. Implementation. Berkeley: University of California Press.

Quadagno, J. 1987. Theories of the welfare state. Annual Review of Sociology 13, 109–28.

_____. 1994. The color of welfare. New York: Oxford University Press.

Rae, D. 1981. Equalities. Cambridge, MA: Harvard University Press.

Rawls, J. 1958. Justice as fairness. Philosophical Review 67, 164–94.

———. 1971. A theory of justice. Oxford: Oxford University Press.

Reference Group on Welfare Reform to the Minister for Social Services. 2015. A new system for better employment and social outcomes. Canberra: Department for Social Services.

Richardson, J. 1960. Economic and financial aspects of social security. London: George Allen and Unwin.

Ryan, A. 1989. Value judgments and welfare, in D. Helm (ed.), The economic borders of the state. Oxford: Oxford University Press.

Saunders, P. 2011. Down and out: poverty and exclusion in Australia. Bristol: Policy Press.

Schatz, S. 1994. Structural adjustment in Africa: a failing grade so far. Journal of Modern African Studies 32(4), 679–92.

Scottish Government. 2015. Creating a fairer Scotland. http://www.gov.scot/Publications/2015/06/4845/downloads#res479666.

Seldon, A. 1977. Charge! London: Temple Smith.

Sen, A. 1993. Markets and freedoms. Oxford Economic Papers 45(4), 519–41.

———. 2001. Development as freedom. Oxford: Oxford University Press.

Smith, A. 1759. The theory of moral sentiments. http://www.econlib.org/library/Smith/smMS.html.

Spencer, H. 1864. Man versus the state. http://www.econlib.org/library/LFBooks/Spencer/spnMvS0.html.

Spicker, P. 1993a. Needs as claims. Social Policy and Administration 27(1), 7–17.

_____. 1993b. Poverty and social security. London: Routledge.

_____. 1996. Normative comparisons of social security systems, in L. Hantrais and S. Mangen (eds.), Cross-national research methods in the social sciences. London: Pinter.

_____. 2002. France, in J. Dixon and R. Scheurell (eds.), The state of social welfare: the twentieth century in cross-national review, 109–24. Westport, CT: Praeger.

_____. 2006a. Liberty, equality, fraternity. Bristol: Policy Press.

_____. 2006b. Policy analysis for practice. Bristol: Policy Press.

_____ 2010. The origins of modern welfare. Oxford: Peter Lang.

_____. 2013. Reclaiming individualism. Bristol: Policy Press.

Standing, G. 2014. The precariat. New York: Bloomsbury.

Starr, R. 1997. General equilibrium theory. Cambridge: Cambridge University Press.

Stuckler, D., and S. Basu. 2013. The body economic. Harmondsworth: Penguin.

Talmud. Tractate Baba Bathra.

Tawney, R. 1930. Equality. London: Allen and Unwin.

Taylor Gooby, P., and T. Larsen. 2004. The UK—a test case for the liberal welfare state? in P. Taylor Gooby (ed.), New risks, new welfare. Oxford: Oxford University Press.

Thaler, R., and C. Sunstein. 2008. Nudge. New Haven, CT: Yale University Press.

Thatcher, M. 1987. Interview for Women's Own. http://www.margaretthatcher.org/document/106689.

Thomson J. (ed.). 1953. The ethics of Aristotle. Harmondsworth: Penguin.

Titmuss, R. 1955. The social division of welfare, in Essays on 'the welfare state'. London: Allen and Unwin, 1963.

———. 1968. Commitment to welfare. London: Allen and Unwin.

———. 1970. The gift relationship. Harmondsworth: Penguin.

———. 1974. Social policy. London: Allen and Unwin.

Townsend, P. 1979. Poverty in the United Kingdom. Harmondsworth: Penguin.

Tudor Hart, J. 1971. The inverse care law, in G. Smith, D. Dorling and M. Shaw (eds.), 2001, Poverty, inequality and health in Britain 1800–2000. Bristol: Policy Press.

United Nations. 1948. Universal declaration of human rights.

———. 2003. Monterrey consensus on financing for development. www.un.org/esa/ffd/monterrey/MonterreyConsensus.pdf.

———. 2012. Guiding principles on extreme poverty and human rights. http://www.ohchr.org/Documents/Publications/OHCHR_ExtremePovertyandHumanRights_EN.pdf.

United Nations Development Programme. 1990. Human development report 1990. New York: United Nations.

United Nations Human Rights Council. 2014. Report of the special rapporteur on the rights of indigenous peoples James Anaya: The situation of indigenous peoples in Canada. http://www.ohchr.org/Documents/Issues/IPeoples/SR/A.HRC.27.52.Add.2.doc.

Veit-Wilson, J. 2000. States of welfare. Social Policy and Administration 34(1), 1–25.

Wagner, G. 1988. Residential care: a positive choice. London: HMSO.

Walby, S. 2004. The European Union and gender equality. Social Politics 11(1), 24–29.

Waldron, J. 1997. Homelessness and the issue of freedom, in R. Goodin and P. Pettit (eds.), Contemporary political philosophy. Oxford: Blackwell.

Whittell, R., and M. Dugan. 2014. Services provider established by outsourcing giant Serco overcharged NHS by millions. Independent, 27 August.

Wilensky, H. 1975. The welfare state and equality. Berkeley: University of California Press.

Wilensky, H., and C. Lebeaux. 1965. Industrial society and social welfare. New York: Free Press.

Wilkinson, R., and K. Pickett. 2009. The spirit level. London: Allen Lane.

Winston, C. 2006. Government failure versus market failure. Washington, DC: Brookings.

Wolf, C. 1978. A theory of non-market failure. Washington, DC: Rand Corporation.

Wontner, T. 1835. Abolition of pauperism. London: Steill.

Woodroofe, K. 1966. From charity to social work. London: Routledge and Kegan Paul.

World Bank. 1993. World development report 1993: investing in health. Washington, DC: World Bank.

———. 1994. Adjustment in Africa: reforms, results and the road ahead. Washington, DC: World Bank.

———. 2009. Social protection. http://go.worldbank.org/R8ABRRLKX0.

World Health Organisation. 2008. Essential health packages. http://www.who.int/healthsystems/topics/delivery/technical_brief_ehp.pdf.

Zezza, G. 2012. The impact of fiscal austerity in the Eurozone, Review of Keynesian Economics 1(1), 37-54.

Index

About the Author

Paul Spicker is Emeritus Professor of Public Policy at the Robert Gordon University, Aberdeen, and a Fellow of CROP, the International Social Science Council's Comparative Research Group on Poverty. His research includes studies of poverty, need, disadvantage and service delivery. He has worked as a consultant for a range of agencies in social welfare provision. His books include *The Welfare State: A General Theory* (2000); *Liberty, Equality and Fraternity* (2006); *Policy Analysis for Practice* (2006); *The Idea of Poverty* (2007); *Poverty: An International Glossary* (co-edited with Sonia Alvarez Leguizamon and David Gordon, 2007); *The Origins of Modern Welfare* (2010); *How Social Security Works* (2011); *Reclaiming Individualism* (2013); *Social Policy: Theory and Practice* (2014); and *What's Wrong with Social Security Benefits?* (2017).